ABUNDANT LIVING

Your Path to Financial Peace and Freedom

Margaret L. Good, CPA

XMS Publishing
1391 NW St Lucie West Blvd, Suite 247
Port St Lucie, FL 34986

ISBN-10: 0692964134
ISBN-13: 978-0692964132

Published in the United States of America

Dedication

This book is dedicated to Yoli - my true friend, sister and anchor in life

TABLE OF CONTENTS

CHAPTER 1 - The Bible and Money

*"The earth and everything on it belong to the Lord.
The world and its people belong to him."*
Psalm 24:1

Prayer: *Lord, today I come to You with everything I have. I lay it at Your feet! Help me to examine my heart, my mind, and my wallet! I give You this time, and ask You to give me strength to do what I need to do to be a good steward. Thank You for all I have, Lord. Amen!*

Money.

"The root of all evil," some people say. "Makes the world go 'round," say others. We all need it; most of us think we need more of it. It's pretty impossible to live without it! We need it to buy food to eat, have a roof over our heads, etc.

Jesus talked about it too, more than just about any other subject; He seemed to take it pretty seriously. Churches talk about it a lot too, sometimes more than we'd like. They seem to ask for it every week, even when we just gave last week!

Our children want it too. So does the government. Bill collectors. Etcetera. And sometimes, it can consume our every waking thought: how do we manage the money we have? Why does it always seem like we don't have enough? How do we get more? How do we hang on to what we've got?

The more we think about it, the more confused we often get. Our parents give us advice, our friends want to chime in, and then the church decides to put its two cents in!

The world absolutely has its views on money: how to get it, and what to do with it. But as believers, it's important that we have a different foundation: what does God say about it? What does the Bible say? Are there biblical principles we can follow that will lead us to financial stability?

The Bible has a lot to say on the subject of money, actually. And Jesus talked about it, more than almost any other topic! Let's look at one of the most famous Bible characters, King David, and see where to begin:

The King stood before the people. They were getting ready to break ground on what was to be the most magnificent temple known to man; God's Spirit had given him the plans! It was to house the most glorious of all—the Ark of the Covenant, the beautiful chest that housed Aaron's rod, the tablets with the Ten Commandments, and a bowl of manna, representing God's history with His people.

He, King David, would not be the one to build the temple. He had planned to build it, but God had told him differently: "You are not to build a house for my Name, because you are a warrior and have shed blood." David accepted this, and today, he was publicly announcing his plan to turn the building of the temple over to his son, Solomon.

The building of this temple would take money—and lots of it. The furniture in the temple was to be made of gold and silver. There were to be precious woods and stones. It was to be the finest structure the world had ever seen, inside and out.

David stood to address the crowd.

"My son Solomon, the one whom God has chosen, is young and inexperienced. The task is great, because this palatial structure is not for man but for the LORD God. With all my resources, I have provided for the temple of my God—gold for the gold work, silver for the silver, bronze for the bronze, iron for the iron and wood for the wood, as well as onyx for the settings, turquoise, stones of various colors, and all kinds of fine stone and marble—all of these in large quantities. Besides, in my devotion to the temple of my God I now give my personal treasures of gold and silver for the temple of my God, over and above everything I have provided for this holy temple: three thousand talents of gold (gold of Ophir) and seven thousand talents of refined silver, for the overlaying of the walls of the buildings, for the gold work and the silver work, and for all the work to be done by the craftsmen. Now, who is willing to consecrate themselves to the LORD today?"

Then the leaders of families, the officers of the tribes of Israel, the commanders of thousands and commanders of hundreds, and the officials in charge of the king's work gave willingly. They gave toward the work on the temple of God five thousand talents and ten thousand darics of gold, ten thousand talents of silver, eighteen thousand talents of bronze and a hundred thousand talents of iron. Anyone who had precious stones gave them to the treasury of the temple of the LORD in the custody of Jehiel the Gershonite. The people rejoiced at the willing response of their leaders, for they had given freely and wholeheartedly *to the LORD. David the king also rejoiced greatly.* [1]

The structure was completed, and it was glorious. King David and the Israelites gave abundantly of their wealth to build God's temple.

Why include a story about an Old Testament king when we are discussing what we need to do with our money today? What could this guy possibly have to do with me, you might ask?

David started out as a shepherd, taking care of his father's flock of sheep while his brothers fought the enemies of Israel. Over time, David grew to be king, and amassed significant wealth. Then King David sacrificed this significant wealth to build a temple someone else would get credit for. He laid down everything he had, and he asked his people to do the same—and they did!

Where did all this abundance come from? How did the Israelites, and David himself, have so much to give? David described in detail how much he had offered, and then he invited the Israelites to do the same! And not only did they do it—they were *happy* about it! How is that possible?

I have something to tell you: we don't actually own anything. Oh, our garages and closets may look like we do (and we pay the bills as if we do). But as Psalm 50 states, *"For every animal of the forest is mine, and the cattle on a thousand hills. I know every bird in the mountains, and the creatures of the field are mine. If I were hungry I would not tell you, **for all the world is mine, and all that is in it**"* (Psalm 50:10-12, emphasis mine).

---

[1] Paraphrased from 1 Chronicles 28-29

God's plan from the beginning was that He would create a marvelous world, and we as His sons and daughters would take care of what He had given us. We call this idea *stewardship,* which means "the responsible overseeing and protection of something considered worth caring for and preserving." [2] We are assigned the care and preservation of what God has provided for us.

James 1:17 says, *"Every good and perfect gift is from above, coming down from the Father of the heavenly lights, who does not change like shifting shadows."* Do you see what that says? *Every* gift. Every single one. There's nothing that we have that didn't come from our heavenly Father. Romans tells us that *"from him and through him and to him are all things* (Romans 11:36). From Him are all things!!

Notice that it says in James that every *good* gift comes from the Father of Lights. You see, we have a very, very good Father, who desires to give us *good things.* Proverbs 10:23 says, *"The blessing of the Lord brings wealth, and he adds no trouble to it."* We have a very generous heavenly Father, who blesses us with wealth! The same Father who knows exactly how many hairs we have on our heads (Luke 12:7) provides everything we need. He is the one who provided all that stuff you have in your garages and closets!

I know many of you may have had negative experiences with your earthly father, but it's so important to know just how good our heavenly Father is. Earlier, I quoted the book of James, which tells us that *"every good and perfect gift"* comes from Him! His heart is to give you

---

[2] Dictionary.com

good things, to fill your life with blessings. He is an abundant, gift-giving Father.

Although He loves us and wants good things for us, His heart is not that we would become hoarders of things, overloaded and overstuffed with *stuff.* One way we can know this is true is that *you can't take it with you when you go.* Any of it. All of us will die someday, and when we do, all of our stuff stays right here.

The Egyptians provide us with a great example of this. In ancient Egyptian culture, when someone died, he or she was often buried with many of his or her favorite possessions: furniture, pots, bowls, clothing. One pharaoh was even buried with a boat! And how do we know they didn't take it with them when they died? Well, the fact that archaeologists were able to dig it up thousands of years later proves that while the person buried in the tomb had gone on to eternity, his or her possessions were still right here on earth.

So if we're not to hoard them, and we can't take them with us, what are we to do with our generous God's abundant blessings? Read this story from Matthew 25:

14 *"Again, it will be like a man going on a journey, who called his servants and entrusted his wealth to them.* 15 *To one he gave five bags of gold, to another two bags, and to another one bag, each according to his ability. Then he went on his journey.* 16 *The man who had received five bags of gold went at once and put his money to work and gained five bags more.* 17 *So also, the one with two bags of gold gained two more.* 18 *But the man who had received one bag went off, dug a hole in the ground and hid his master's money.*

¹⁹ "After a long time the master of those servants returned and settled accounts with them. ²⁰ The man who had received five bags of gold brought the other five. 'Master,' he said, 'you entrusted me with five bags of gold. See, I have gained five more.'

²¹ "His master replied, 'Well done, good and faithful servant! You have been faithful with a few things; I will put you in charge of many things. Come and share your master's happiness!'

²² "The man with two bags of gold also came. 'Master,' he said, 'you entrusted me with two bags of gold; see, I have gained two more.'

²³ "His master replied, 'Well done, good and faithful servant! You have been faithful with a few things; I will put you in charge of many things. Come and share your master's happiness!'

²⁴ "Then the man who had received one bag of gold came. 'Master,' he said, 'I knew that you are a hard man, harvesting where you have not sown and gathering where you have not scattered seed. ²⁵ So I was afraid and went out and hid your gold in the ground. See, here is what belongs to you.'

²⁶ "His master replied, 'You wicked, lazy servant! So you knew that I harvest where I have not sown and gather where I have not scattered seed? ²⁷ Well then, you should have put my money on deposit with the bankers, so that when I returned I would have received it back with interest.

²⁸ "'So take the bag of gold from him and give it to the one who has ten bags. ²⁹ For whoever has will be given more, and they will have an abundance. Whoever does not have, even what they have will be taken from them. ³⁰ And throw that worthless servant outside, into the darkness, where there will be weeping and gnashing of teeth.'

The man who buried his treasure lost everything. (It's also important to notice that he was the man who called the Master a "hard man;" he did not understand the Father's generous heart!) We are to *steward* God's blessings, multiplying them and distributing them to others.

Our very generous Father takes this pretty seriously. Read what Proverbs has to say: *"Whoever shuts their ears to the cry of the poor will also cry out and not be answered"* (Proverbs 21:13). What would it mean to "shut our ears" to the cry of the poor? It would mean not using our resources to help others less fortunate than we are. When He gives us things, He intends for us to use those things to bless others and advance his Kingdom. He blesses us so that we in turn can be a blessing to others.

God also asks us to give back to our local church body; we call it "tithing." The principle of tithing looks like this: God gives us 100% of what we have, and asks that we return 10% of it back to our church.

But God is so good, that even in asking us to tithe, He makes us promises! Look at this: *"Bring the whole tithe into the storehouse, that there may be food in my house. Test me in this," says the* L*ORD* *Almighty, "and see if I will not throw open the floodgates of heaven and pour out so much blessing that there will not be room enough to store it. I will prevent pests from devouring your crops, and the vines in your fields will not drop their fruit before it is ripe," says the* L*ORD* *Almighty. "Then all the nations will call you blessed, for yours will be a delightful land," says the* L*ORD* *Almighty'"* (Malachi 3:10). When we follow his instructions to tithe on what He's given us, he will open the floodgates of heaven!

This is also the one area where God gives us permission to "test" Him: *"see if I won't do it,"* He says. Nowhere else are we commanded to test Him and His faithfulness. But in this area, He actually invites us to do it!

You may be wondering, "What is a *tithe?"* A tithe is defined as 1/10th of your income, given back to the Lord. Leviticus 27:30 says, *"'A tithe of everything from the land, whether grain from the soil or fruit from the trees, belongs to the LORD; it is holy to the LORD."* Most people believe it should be the first tenth, the first thing you do with your money after getting paid. We'll talk more about it later in this book, but Scripture shows us that because God is a good God, and everything comes from Him, that we should return a portion of it to Him.

You see, everything we have comes from God, and is to be returned to Him to be used for His purposes. It's all His anyway!

Throughout this book, we will examine God's heart about money—and our own. We will dig into our money personalities, our budgets (or lack thereof), our savings plans, and how we can leave a legacy for the next generation. It will be hard sometimes; we tend to get a little weird about money, don't we? We don't like people digging into our finances, or our heart about them. We may get defensive, and you may ask, "Who are you, Margaret, to ask me all these questions about *my money?"*

If you're reading this book, it's likely because you've found yourself in a place where you absolutely have to examine your finances. Maybe you're in a crisis, and you don't know how to get out. Or maybe you're not in crisis yet—but you know you're headed for one.

Or maybe you're just starting out in life, and you're ready to build a foundation of financial security. Wherever you are, we're on this journey together. Today is the first day of your future!
Ready? Let's go!

HOMEWORK:

Matthew 6:21 says, *"For where your treasure is, there your heart will be also."* We've quoted that backwards sometimes, thinking that what we love is where we will spend our money or time or energy. And that's true, but if you look at what the actual verse says, it shows that we can look at where we spend our time or money or energy to find out where our heart is!

In the Appendix of this book, you will find a worksheet entitled **"Personal Cash Position."** This worksheet is designed to give you a snapshot of where you are financially, right now.

For your homework this week, take the worksheet and your personal bank statement and begin to categorize your spending. Make sure you're categorizing not just your credit or debit card expenditures, but your cash spending. If you don't normally track your cash spending, now would be a good time to begin to track that.

I suggest getting a small notebook, and beginning to track all of your spending. Make sure you write down everything—that cup of coffee at the gas station, the quick run through the drive-thru, the extra magazine at the grocery store. You might be surprised at how much you're spending at Tim Horton's or Starbucks, a dollar here or five dollars there. It adds up!

CHAPTER 2 - The Heart of the Matter

Rejoice always, pray continually, give thanks in all circumstances; for this is God's will for you in Christ Jesus.
1 Thessalonians 5:16-18

Prayer: *Lord, examine my heart. Show me where my thoughts and beliefs are out of line with Yours. Help me know how to take care of my heart and my money, all at the same time! You are a good Father! Lord, help me trust You more! Amen.*

We've talked a bit about how God sees money. Now it's important to explore how we humans look at it.

Jesus taught in parables, stories meant to reveal truth about God and about humans. In Luke 12, Jesus tells this parable:

 13 Someone in the crowd said to him, "Teacher, tell my brother to divide the inheritance with me."
*14 Jesus replied, "Man, who appointed me a judge or an arbiter between you?" 15 Then he said to them, "**Watch out! Be on your guard against all kinds of greed; life does not consist in an abundance of possessions.**"*
16 And he told them this parable: "The ground of a certain rich man yielded an abundant harvest. 17 He thought to himself, 'What shall I do? I have no place to store my crops.'
18 "Then he said, 'This is what I'll do. I will tear down my barns and build bigger ones, and there I will store my surplus grain. 19 And I'll say to myself, "You have plenty of grain laid up for many years. Take life easy; eat, drink and

be merry." '

²⁰ *"But God said to him, 'You fool! This very night your life will be demanded from you. Then who will get what you have prepared for yourself?'*

²¹ *"This is how it will be with whoever stores up things for themselves but is not rich toward God."* (Luke 12:13-21, emphasis mine)

There are two principles we can learn from this parable. One, Jesus warns us about greed. The dictionary defines greed as "excessive ... desire, especially for wealth or possessions." Jesus knows how we are as humans, how we have a tendency to want more and more, to not be satisfied with what we have.

Have you ever felt that way? I have. When I see that new house, or that new car, or that new piece of furniture or jewelry, and I just have to have it—even when I have a perfectly good house, or car, or couch. Does that mean we should never want new things? Of course not. Greed is not about what you buy; it's about the condition of your heart.

You see, a heart that doesn't know that he or she is the child of a very good, very generous Father will always strive to get more, to have more, to find their sense of significance or worth in having things and more things. A greedy heart will never have enough money in its bank account—no matter how many zeros it may have.

Jesus knew this about us, which is why He gave us the parable above. *"Life does not consist in an abundance of possessions,"* He says, and then tells a story of a man who does just that—looks for his life in a big pile of stuff.

Secondly, Jesus tells us, just a few pages past this parable in Luke 17, that *"whoever tries to keep their life will lose it"* (v. 33). Jesus knew that the human heart, apart from God, is never satisfied; it is always hungry, always wanting more. The second half of that verse says this: *"whoever loses their life will preserve it."* Does that mean we should lie down and die? Of course not! Jesus simply means that when we spend all of our time worrying about our own needs and wants, we cannot focus on what God has for us to do here on earth.

Jesus continues:

"22 Then Jesus said to his disciples: "Therefore I tell you, do not worry about your life, what you will eat; or about your body, what you will wear. 23 For life is more than food, and the body more than clothes. 24 Consider the ravens: They do not sow or reap, they have no storeroom or barn; yet God feeds them. And how much more valuable you are than birds! 25 Who of you by worrying can add a single hour to your life? 26 Since you cannot do this very little thing, why do you worry about the rest?" (Luke 12:22-25) *Don't worry,* Jesus says! Don't worry?? you say. How can I not worry? Have you seen the pile of bills stacking up, or the payment coming due?

How we look at money is never really about money, is it? I can have very little money, and yet have everything I need and be content. Or I can have lots of money, more than I know what to do with, and yet always be hungry for more—and vice versa! It's about our heart. Jesus knew this. So what do we do? When I find myself feeling greedy and dissatisfied, how do I help my heart?

First of all, you need to understand that you have control over your own heart. If we didn't, why would we need to be reminded to "guard" it? As Proverbs 4:23 states, *"Above all else, guard your heart, for everything you do flows from it."* God is asking YOU to take charge over your own heart, to put guardrails around what you think and feel—because everything you do flows from your heart.

The writer of Hebrews says it this way: *"Keep your lives free from the love of money and be content with what you have"* (Hebrews 13:5). Does it say to keep your lives free from money? Of course not. But it *does* say to keep your life free from the *"love of money."* Where do we love? In our hearts. We are to steward our hearts in such a way that we do not fall in love with money and what we think it can do for us.

The book of Ecclesiastes is an interesting book, written by King Solomon. Many scholars believe that Solomon was the richest man who ever lived. He had more money, more property, more jewels than anyone—and this is the man who wrote: *"Whoever loves money never has enough; whoever loves wealth is never satisfied with their income"* (Ecclesiastes 5:10).

Solomon was also considered the wisest man who ever lived. As a man who had everything he could ever want or need—and more—he understood that the love of money, that greed, will never be enough. It will never satisfy.

So what do we do? We can guard *against* things, but is there anything we can do proactively?

One of the primary ways we can guard our hearts against greed and cultivate a proper perspective on money and possessions is by practicing one simple thing:

Gratitude.

Thankfulness. Being thankful. Being aware that as we stated earlier, *every good and perfect gift* comes from God. In all things give thanks.

This can truly be a challenge. Two weeks before our first house closed I was laid off from my job with a software company which merged with another. They no longer needed two accounting departments and since I was the last one hired, only eight months before, I was the one to be laid off.

To be honest, it was a blessing. I didn't like my job or the company. I had toyed around in my head about leaving and going out on my own. I knew exactly what I wanted to do but I lacked the courage to do it. In God's wisdom, He gave me the push I needed to move forward and live the dream that I had. There were a few challenges along the way since our mortgage and lifestyle were based on two full time professional incomes but God always provided. We never worried about food, clothing or shelter. He always looked after us. It truly was an experience to be thankful for since I would most likely not have been where I am today.

To this day, I have a plaque by my desk that says, "in all things give thanks to the Lord." He truly has the master plan and we have to trust Him with all our heart because He knows what's best for us.

Thankfulness actually positions us to receive from God, because it changes what we focus on. If I'm complaining about what I don't have all the time, how will I be able to see what God is actually doing in my life? Being thankful allows me to focus on what I already have—and be grateful for it.

We have so many blessings in our lives! Most of you reading this will have woken up this morning under a solid roof, in a warm bed, with hot running water and toilets that flush. These are good things! We can be thankful for them! Maybe you have a family, or good friends. A car that works, and a job to go to.
Or maybe you don't have those things.

1 Thessalonians tells us to give thanks in *all circumstances*. That can be hard, can't it? It has been for me.

But God truly knows what is best for us. When pursuing my CPA career I worked for a very large accounting firm. The pressures were constant. Had I stayed with the firm I would have been working 80 hour weeks and trying to climb the ladder to partnership status. Initially, that was my dream. I loved my work but the chemical imbalance that the stress caused me prohibited me from continuing the pursuit of my dream. The failure to realize my dream my way was crushing and almost put me over the edge.

Over time, God has shown me how to manage my stressors and to focus on what He wants for my life. I'm thankful that God showed me early in my career that He was to be my focus. Whenever I have taken my eyes off Him, sure enough the stress comes back because I try to accomplish the task at hand on my own instead of waiting on the Lord. So now I know if I am stressing, it's a sign that I have taken my eyes of the Lord and am not trusting Him with all my heart, that I'm trying to do it all my way. Thankfully I learnt this lesson but it did take me a few trips to wake up to what the Lord really wanted: my undivided attention.

Practicing thankfulness also reminds us that not all of our blessings are *things.* The sound of rain on the roof when you have nowhere to go, a fresh snowfall, the first sounds of the birds in spring ... these are all joys our Father has set before us.

But our greatest treasure is always people. If you're married, your spouse is a treasure. If you have children, they are treasures. Your friends. Your church family. Your parents (yes, really!). The love and friendship you share with the people in your life is one of the greatest joys you could ever experience.

Practice thanking God for them! Thank Him for them first thing in the morning, then again before you go to sleep at night. Practice thanking Him for the beautiful blue sky, for the flowers in the field, for the people in your world.

But we don't get along, you might say. I'm mad at my spouse/kids/church/whatever. What would happen if you practiced thankfulness for those people? What if you woke up every morning, thanking God for your spouse? How might that change your relationship? Would it be worth it to find out?

It's easy to be grateful for some things, and harder for others. But if *every good and perfect gift* comes from our good Father, shouldn't we thank Him for all of them?

Gratitude can also help when we feel anxious about money. It turns our hearts from focusing on what we think God isn't doing, and refocuses them on what He is doing. As Jesus continues in Luke 12, *"'Consider how the wild flowers grow. They do not labor or spin. Yet I tell you, not even Solomon in all his splendor was dressed like one of these. If that is how God clothes the grass of the field, which is here today, and tomorrow is thrown into the fire, how much more will he clothe you—you of little faith! And do not set your heart on what you will eat or drink; do not worry about it. For the pagan world runs after all such things, and your Father knows that you need them. But seek his kingdom, and these things will be given to you as well'"* (Luke 12:27-31).

As we talk about money and possessions and what to do with them, I challenge you to cultivate an "attitude of gratitude." Practice being thankful; you might be surprised at what you see!

HOMEWORK:

1. Start a "Gratitude Journal." Find a notebook or a journal of some kind; it doesn't have to be fancy. Every night before you go to sleep, write down in your journal the date and five things you are grateful for that day.

   It could be as simple as being grateful for the water we drink or the roof over our heads. If you can become more specific about things that would be good.

   It can initially be a bit daunting to think about five things; what am I going to write about? What am

I going to say? You don't want to repeat yourself. You will notice that when you think about what you're grateful for, they can be small things. For example, for someone: your child, your husband, your wife, your grandchildren. For someone at work who had done something for you, bought you coffee when they didn't have to, opened the door for you.

Anything! Having your favorite ice cream. Watching a good movie. Reading a good book (like this one!).

Don't worry about how many items you need to have. Just get started, focusing on the positives. You may find you can write more than five!

2. In your homework from Chapter 1, you began tracking your spending. This week, take that a step further.

Make sure that your tracking journal matches up with your bank statement.

If you haven't yet categorized your spending, do that now. (The "**Personal Cash Position**" worksheet is in the Appendix of this book.)

Pull your bank statement. Most banks now have online access. If you haven't figured that out yet, contact your bank and figure out how to get into your account. Take some time and read over how your statement is laid out: are your debits (withdrawals) in red, and your deposits in black? Does it list your expenditures by date? If you have a joint account with separate debit cards, does your statement allow you to see which card is used where?

Get familiar with your banking statement. This is a great time to notice any   hidden fees your bank might be charging you. If you spot something you don't   understand, call your local branch. They should be able to discuss things with you, and maybe even help you determine if you're using the right type of account   for your needs.

Be honest with yourself. Just like a dieter sometimes wants to "cheat," it can   be easy to overlook small expenditures. Write them all down! We will do more with this information later on; right now, this exercise is to give you a glimpse into where you are spending your money—and where your heart is.

CHAPTER 3 - Tithing and Giving

"Trust in the Lord with all your heart and lean not on your own understanding; in all your ways submit to him, and he will make your paths straight."
Proverbs 3:5-6

Prayer: *Lord, You are good! Your ways are higher than my ways! Help me to trust You more. Help me to hold everything You've given me with open hands, trusting You with what you ask me to do with it. I know that You will take care of me, that You will always meet my needs. Thank You for Your great faithfulness! Amen.*

As Christians, we talk a lot about "faith"—what it is, how we get it, and why we should have it. Hebrews tells us it's the "substance" of what we hope for, the "evidence" of what we can't see—and that without it, it's impossible to please God.

So what is it? The word "faith" can be most accurately defined as "firm persuasion." I have *faith* that gravity works; I am *firmly persuaded* (perhaps by many falls or accidents) that it does. I have faith that the sun will come up every morning. I am firmly persuaded that (unless I haven't paid the bill) my light will come on when I flip the switch.

For us as believers in Christ, we must be firmly persuaded *"that he is, and that he is a rewarder of those who seek him"* (Hebrews 11:6). In other words, we have to be absolutely convinced of who Jesus is, and how He relates to us. This is why it's so important to get to know Him, and to get to know God as a good Father.

21

The book of James, though, tells us that *"faith without deeds is dead"* (James 2:26). We can say that we have faith, but our actions will show whether we do or not, and there's no greater place to see this than in our finances.

In chapter 2, we talked about how good God is, how generous He is, and that He will never leave us or forsake us. Those are all good things to say, but the question is, do you trust Him with your money? Do you trust Him— who gives all good gifts—to take care of you?

The Bible gives us examples of people that showed great faith.

A large crowd followed and pressed around him. 25 And a woman was there who had been subject to bleeding for twelve years. 26 She had suffered a great deal under the care of many doctors and had spent all she had, yet instead of getting better she grew worse. 27 When she heard about Jesus, she came up behind him in the crowd and touched his cloak, 28 because she thought, "If I just touch his clothes, I will be healed." 29 Immediately her bleeding stopped and she felt in her body that she was freed from her suffering. 30 At once Jesus realized that power had gone out from him. He turned around in the crowd and asked, "Who touched my clothes?" 31 "You see the people crowding against you," his disciples answered, "and yet you can ask, 'Who touched me?'"

32 But Jesus kept looking around to see who had done it. 33 Then the woman, knowing what had happened to her, came and fell at his feet and, trembling with fear, told him the whole truth. 34 He said to her, "Daughter, your faith has healed you. Go in peace and be freed from your suffering." (Mark 5:24-34)

This woman showed great faith! Despite her suffering, and despite the crowds, and despite the fact that the people around her would have known who she was and what she suffered from (and as a result would have shunned her), she was *firmly convinced* that if she could just get to Jesus, she would be healed. And she was.

Luke tells another story of great faith:

> *17 One day Jesus was teaching, and Pharisees and teachers of the law were sitting there. They had come from every village of Galilee and from Judea and Jerusalem. And the power of the Lord was with Jesus to heal the sick. 18 Some men came carrying a paralyzed man on a mat and tried to take him into the house to lay him before Jesus. 19 When they could not find a way to do this because of the crowd, they went up on the roof and lowered him on his mat through the tiles into the middle of the crowd, right in front of Jesus.20 When Jesus saw their faith, he said, "Friend, your sins are forgiven."*
> (Luke 5:17-20)

This man's friends knew that Jesus would heal him. They just knew it! And so they did what was necessary to get him to Jesus.

It's important to see that faith isn't about an outcome. The woman with the issue of blood had probably been stepped on, bumped, knocked about, and probably worse. But her only thought was to get to Jesus, no matter what. Her circumstances drove her there, but her faith was in Jesus Himself, and who she believed Him to be.

That is faith. That is what "pleases" God, that we will do whatever it takes to get to Him because we are so firmly convinced of His presence and His goodness.

It's easy to talk about faith by telling Bible stories and praying for someone to get healed. But maybe it's not so easy to talk about faith when we start talking about money.

If you've been in church for a while, you've probably heard someone mention the word "tithing." Maybe they say something like, "It's time now to take up our tithes and offerings." Or, "Don't forget to leave your tithe on the way out of church today!" Maybe you've heard of it, but you don't really know what it is.

Malachi 3:10 says, *"Bring the whole tithe into the storehouse, that there may be food in my house."* That word "tithe" literally means "a tenth." So the command here is to give a tenth of your income, into the "storehouse." This is God speaking; He commands that the tithe be brought into the storehouse—*"that there may be food in **my** house"* (emphasis added). Whose house? God's house!

The "house" of the Lord is His church! God's plan is to work through His church to bring about His plans on the earth; well, as with any house, it does take money to make things happen. It takes money, just to turn the lights on! God's plan is that His church would do His work on the earth—and that His people would fund it through their tithes and offerings. Remember the story of the temple from chapter 1? The building of the temple was funded by the King—and by the people giving generously!

Where should you tithe? Ideally, you should tithe to the

local church you attend regularly. If you don't have a local church body, then tithe to the ministry you receive the most from. Do you listen to podcasts from a particular church? Do you read books written by the pastors? Send your tithe to that church, as a return on what you have received from them.

But I can't afford 10%, you might say. For many people who are just getting started on their journey to healthy finances find that to tithe 10% of their income to the church would mean they can't pay other bills, or sometimes even buy groceries to feed their families. So if you're in that situation, what can you do?

Some teachers have taught that if you don't tithe 10%, your other 90% will be "cursed." I disagree with this. I can't see how a good, loving Father would "curse" His children! Is His heart for you to tithe? Of course! The rest of Malachi 3:10 explains why:

And thereby put me to the test, says the LORD of hosts, if I will not open the windows of heaven for you and pour down for you a blessing until there is no more need.

His heart is to bless His children! His heart is to open the windows of heaven for you! So what can you do? If you don't think 10% is possible right now, why not start with 5%? Or 3%? The point is, start somewhere. Even a little bit will get you moving in the right direction! Start small, and then work your way up to 10%--or more! I know church leaders who tithe at least 20%. Of course that's not required, but what a goal to aspire to!

Many people view paying their tithe the same way they view their rent, or their electric bill. They pay it first, as soon as they receive their paycheck. That way it doesn't accidentally get spent on other things. If your paycheck is the same every month, you might consider setting up an automatic draft for your tithe.

Another question that might arise is should you tithe on your "gross" income (what you make before taxes or other things are taken out) or your "net" income (what you actually see on your paycheck). If you think about it, your gross income is the money you have actually earned, so your tithe would be 10% of that amount.

"Why does the church need my money," you might ask? Think of it this way. If you attend church, the church very likely meets in a building that they either have a mortgage on, or are paying rent for. Then, as with any building, there are utilities that have to be paid: electricity, water (hard to imagine going to church without the ability to use the restroom, yes?), perhaps internet. The building itself will need to be kept in good repair, from light bulbs being changed to paint and floor repairs, among others.

Then, besides the building, it takes people to run a church. "Why don't they just volunteer," you say? Many do. But most pastors spend hours every week preparing sermons, meeting with people, studying the Bible, and other countless tasks.

And if you have children, you have likely dropped them off in a child-care-like setting, with trained and vetted workers taking good care of your precious cargo. Very likely, those teachers have spent time during the week preparing lessons, and preparing the classrooms to receive your children. Is that worth some compensation?

Let's not forget the musicians! Most musicians spend hours a week practicing their instruments, and preparing the song lists for the weekend services.

Of course, many many people do this as volunteers out of the kindness of their hearts, but for those of us that attend church, and benefit from these services, it's helpful to provide some compensation for those folks who work hard to make your church-going experience a good one.

So where would that money come from, to run a building and compensate a staff? What about outreaches into the community? Or benevolence funds, accounts that most churches have to be able to take care of their members and others when they need it? How do we fund those things?

Through giving. Through tithes and offerings. God's plan is that His Kingdom would be advanced through the local church, and it takes money for that to happen.
"Hold on," you say. What about that preacher on TV? He asks for money every time he's on there. And the news just had a report about his brand new airplane!

While it's true that there are indeed dishonest people out there who really are just scamming you for your money, most pastors and leaders are just trying to make a living doing something God has gifted them to do—just like you are. For me, giving and tithing has often been more about the condition of my heart than the ministry I gave money to. God was asking me if my faith actually meant that I would trust Him, not only with my finances, but with the character of the people in the ministry.

God is always after our hearts, and how we deal with money is no different.

HOMEWORK:

1. Revisit your Gratitude Journal. Take some time and look through your entries. What stands out to you? Do you see yourself being grateful for little things? Big things? What about people?

Have you been able to come up with five things a day? If not, make that your goal for this week. If so, see if you can add one or two more to your daily list!

2. Keep working on tracking your spending. You should be categorizing your spending, and if you haven't begun using it yet, take some time and fill out the **Personal Cash Position** worksheet in the Appendix. By now, you should have at least a couple of weeks to categorize, and you may start to see some trends in your spending. Begin to examine areas where you might be able to tighten it up a little bit, lowering your spending.

3. In the Appendix, there is a worksheet called **Exercising Our Faith in God.** The very first action item is about anxiety. Philippians 4:6 tells us, *"Do not be anxious about anything, but in every situation, by prayer and petition, with thanksgiving, present your requests to God."* What are you anxious about this week? What is on your mind? This verse tells us what to do with those things, and the very next verse tells us what God will do: *"And the peace of God, which transcends all understanding, will guard your hearts and your minds in Christ Jesus"* (v. 7).

Take some time and examine what makes you anxious. Then hand it over to God! Ask Him for how He wants you to do that—and then trust Him, that He will do what He said!

CHAPTER 4 - The Value of Work

"Do not conform to the pattern of this world, but be transformed by the renewing of your mind. Then you will be able to test and approve what God's will is—his good, pleasing and perfect will."
Romans 12:2

Prayer: *Lord, thank You that I have strength to work! Thank You for the opportunity to work hard, to be satisfied in my work, and to enjoy the fruit of it! I commit today to lean into my work, no matter what it is. Give me strength to do my very best, to honor You in everything I do. Amen.*

There are no get-rich-quick schemes, although people will tell you differently. They'll tell you stories of their supplements and soap, and how they're going to retire young with a big house and a vacation boat. And some of them may actually make a decent profit from those things. But there's one thing they're not telling you. In order to make money in those businesses, as with any business, there's just one way to be successful.

Work.

Perhaps you'll see pictures on social media of your friends on Hawaiian vacations, or in their brand new car. What you don't see is the hours and hours of hard work they have put in to build their networks, market their products, and manage their teams. They may not show you the hours spent in a classroom, learning (or teaching!) their craft or trade, honing their skills.

Part of what has come to be known as the "American Dream" (my Canadian readers will understand this too) is something of a pie-in-the-sky "plan" for retirement: big house, nice cars, vacations, etc.—all paid for, of course. Maybe a few rounds of golf every Tuesday lunch, Disney vacations with the grandkids once a year, etc. There's nothing wrong with this picture; but so many have this dream without fully understanding what they need to do to make it happen.

They need to *work.*

Many people seem to pick up somewhere that money should just be handed to them, and they shouldn't have to work for it. Maybe you know people like that ... nothing you say will change their mind. Maybe you've thought that a time or two; maybe you even bought a lottery ticket, hoping all your troubles would be over.

But that's not how we're designed. When God created Adam, He designed him to work. Genesis 2:15 says, *"The LORD God took the man and put him in the Garden of Eden to **work it and take care of it**"*(emphasis mine). This is before the Fall, before any curses and before Adam and Eve had to leave the Garden. This verse actually takes place before Eve is revealed; God creates Adam, places him in the Garden of Eden, and tells him to work.

In chapter 1, we talked about King David and the building of the temple. Have you ever seen a building being constructed? There is work to be done! Lots of it! God's desire for us is that we would find work fulfilling, that we would take a sense of pride in what we do that can also provide for our needs.

But I don't like my job, you might say. That's ok!

I have had several jobs I haven't liked. But I was thankful for them since they helped lead me to where my true gifts and talents are. So ask yourself, "Why am I in this job I don't like?" Do you really think God wants you to be unhappy in the task you are doing for at least 40 hours a week? I certainly don't. What is the point of your present job? Is it to pay the bills? Take trips? Glorify God? What would you like to do and why aren't you doing it?

Part of exercising stewardship is not just what we do with our resources, but how we obtain those resources to begin with. In Matthew 25, Jesus tells the story of a man who went on a trip. Before he left, he entrusted a few of his workers with some of his resources. When he came back from the trip, he found that two of them had doubled what he had given them—but the third man had buried his employer's resources, not using them to make a profit. The employer is angry with this employee; how dare he misuse the employer's resources, not using them to make a profit? He calls his employee "wicked and lazy," takes the money that he had away from him, and has him thrown out "into the darkness, where there will be wailing and gnashing of teeth."

Sound like fun?

One of the many things Jesus is teaching through this parable is that that we are responsible for stewarding the things God has given us—including our ability to work and make money. It's how He provides for us!

Of course, there are many stories of God's miraculous financial provision for His children. He's a God who rescues, after all! But His heart for us is that we would learn to be hard workers, diligent and faithful in every opportunity.

I love doing needlework. I could do it 24/7. I really wanted my needlework business to be successful. The challenge was that no one valued the artwork enough for me to make a living at it. I much preferred it though to doing accounting even though I was trained and very gifted at accounting. God however helped me do both. My needlework business grew by selling supplies to other needlework lovers. I got to make lots of samples, which didn't themselves sell but were used to sell the patterns, frames and other materials used to make the samples. I used my accounting and business background to analyze my business and my creative side to grow it.

Very often, when we think of God "providing" for us, the picture we have in our heads is one of a miracle: a check in the mail, an unexpected inheritance, a sudden bank error in our favor. And God does indeed use all of these things to provide for us! But the main way God has chose to provide for His children is through their ability to work, and work hard! All of us have gifts and talents, and all of us have the ability to work hard at something.

The writer of the book of Proverbs says it this way:

> Go to the ant, you sluggard;
>   consider its ways and be wise!
> It has no commander,
>   no overseer or ruler,
> yet it stores its provisions in summer
>   and gathers its food at harvest.
>
> How long will you lie there, you sluggard?

When will you get up from your sleep?
A little sleep, a little slumber,
*   a little folding of the hands to rest—*
and poverty will come on you like a thief. (Proverbs
        6:6)

Paul, in his second letter to the Thessalonians, is very clear. In chapter 3, verse 10, he says, *"The one who is unwilling to work shall not eat."* Sounds harsh, you might say. Let's go back a little further in that passage, and see what Paul is talking about here.

"In the name of the Lord Jesus Christ, we command you, brothers and sisters, to keep away from every believer who is idle and disruptive and does not live according to the teaching you received from us. ⁷ For you yourselves know how you ought to follow our example. We were not idle when we were with you, ⁸ nor did we eat anyone's food without paying for it. On the contrary, we worked night and day, laboring and toiling so that we would not be a burden to any of you. ⁹ We did this, not because we do not have the right to such help, but in order to offer ourselves as a model for you to imitate. ¹⁰ For even when we were with you, we gave you this rule: "The one who is unwilling to work shall not eat."
¹¹ We hear that some among you are idle and disruptive. They are not busy; they are busybodies. ¹² Such people we command and urge in the Lord Jesus Christ to settle down and earn the food they eat. ¹³ And as for you, brothers and sisters, never tire of doing what is good."
    (2 Thessalonians 3:6-13)

You see, Paul is encouraging the believers at the church in Thessaloniki to not be idle, to not eat without paying— and to not be a burden to anyone. There are times, of course, when we cannot work: illness, injury, other extenuating circumstances. (In later chapters, we will discuss how to prepare for such times.) But Paul is very clear here: if you can work, you should.

I have counseled people who come with bills they can't pay and no food on the table. When I ask them what they do for a living, sometimes they want to give me excuses about why they can't work; they just want someone else to hand them money. But unless they take responsibility for their own work, they will be right back in front of me (or someone else) looking for a handout.
One of the key first steps to taking control of your finances is just that—taking control. Being responsible. Owning up to the mistakes you have made, recognizing your bad habits—and then doing something about it.

I once counseled a young man who was struggling financially. He had gotten a degree from university, but couldn't find a job in his chosen field. He had dwindled his savings, and now found himself needing help. When I mentioned that the local grocery was hiring, he smirked. "I have a degree," he said. "I'm worth more than the minimum wage they would want to pay me!"

In the end, he wouldn't take my advice. I don't know what happened to him, but I wish he had listened to me. Sometimes, you just need to take a job. It might not be your dream job, and it might not be very high paying. But sometimes just taking a job, no matter how menial it might seem, sets a different momentum in motion. It often takes having a job to get a job (I know how odd that seems, but it's true). Employers like to see whether or not someone will work before they hire them!

We were designed to work. It's a huge part of God's way of providing for us!

If you are already employed, resolve today to do the best job you possibly can. Work hard for your employer "as unto the Lord," whether you wait tables, make coffee, analyze spreadsheets, or teach children to read. Decide that your job is important because you do it.

If you are currently unemployed, begin the process of searching for a job. Look around when you go to local businesses and see if they're hiring. Look online for job openings in your area. Let friends know that you're looking; I can't overstate the value of networking! You never know what opportunities are out there!

Begin to shape a new future. It's impossible to be a good steward of your finances without understanding the value of work. You are powerful! Go and shift the momentum today!

HOMEWORK:

1. Continue with your Gratitude Journal. If you haven't been writing in it every day, make a commitment to being more consistent.

If you have been consistent, try to increase the number of items you write down! Have you been coming up with five? Go for ten! There's no limit to the amount of gratitude you can cultivate!

2. If you already have a job, take a few minutes and journal your thoughts and feelings about your current position. Are there ways in which you could cultivate an "attitude of gratitude" about

your job? Spend some time this week examining how you are approaching your job

3. If you don't have a job, let's go on a job hunt!

Set a goal to put in a few applications this week. Start to look around at who is hiring in your area. Ask a few friends if they know of anything. And then set your goal: is it five? Ten? By this time next week, you'll likely have at least had an initial interview!

Next, examine your closet. Do you have the appropriate clothes for an interview? Make sure you have what you need. If you don't, check around in your area for an upscale resale shop of some kind, or ask friends and family to help you put together an outfit. You'll need to look your best for your upcoming interviews!

Then, follow through! Make some phone calls. Dig around online. Polish up your resume! (See my resume template at the back of the book if you need help creating one.) Fill out applications. Send in resumes.

CHAPTER 5 – Budgeting and a Long-Term Plan

*The plans of the righteous are just, but the
advice of the wicked is deceitful.*
Proverbs 12:5

PRAYER: *Lord, I submit my ways to You: my plans, my
budget, my job, all my hopes and dreams. I know that
anything You have planned for me is so much better than
anything I could plan for myself! Today I choose to give you
everything! Amen!*

It's kind of amazing that we are this far into a book about
money, and we haven't yet discussed budgeting. But
before we talk about what to do with money, it was
important to examine our thinking *about* money. Now
that we've straightened that out, we can get down to
brass tacks.

The dictionary defines a budget in a few different ways:

1. an estimate, often itemized, of expected income
    and expense for a given period in the future.
2. a plan of operations based on such an estimate.
3. an itemized allotment of funds, time, etc., for a
    given period.
4. the total sum of money set aside or needed for a
    purpose: *the construction budget.*
5. a limited stock or supply of something: *his budget
    of goodwill.*

We can say we are "budgeting" for a specific purpose; in

other words, we are planning how much money we will spend on that purpose. To put it simply, a budget is a plan for your money.

Why do we need a budget? Can't we just trust God, and everything will fall into place?

That's not how this works. That's not how any of this works.

As we discussed before, there is a part of this that only God can do. He is your provider. He is the one who owns the cattle on a thousand hills, and all good gifts come from Him. However, He has put you in charge of what to do with what He's given you! That's what "stewardship" actually means, to "steward" or take care of what God has given to you. A budget is one of the primary ways we do that.

A budget is a wonderful tool. A budget can:

- provide a written record of your money, both income and how you spend it
- help with communication
- help you visualize and realize your goals
- reflect your spending habits

Let's take a closer look at these.

A good budget will provide you with a written record of your money, how much comes in, and how much goes out. I don't know about you, but I can't always trust the math in my head. I think I know what is going where, but I very often forget about things. Having a written budget helps me to see everything on paper, in black and white.

Speaking of seeing it in black and white, having a budget helps you with communication. Let's say you're married. One day your spouse comes to you.

"Sweetheart!" he/she says. "Guess what? I just got back from the car lot—" uh-oh "—and the guy there said he can give me a *great deal* on a *brand new car!* And it's the one I've really wanted!"

Just think how handy it would be to calmly walk your spouse over to where your budget is saved (whether on your computer or in a paper file somewhere), open it up, and remind your beloved spouse just how much is in your budget, and whether or not you can afford the *great deal* on the *brand new car.* (We will discuss both car shopping and budgeting as a married couple elsewhere.) It makes the decision a matter of the budget saying no, rather than one spouse or the other.

Having a good budget can help you visualize—and then realize—your goals. We'll discuss goal setting in a minute, but for the purposes of this discussion, let's say you have set a financial goal of buying a house. You have dreams of a big backyard where your dog can run free, where you can park that RV (that's also in your goals). You have an entire Pinterest board dedicated to "what I'll do when I own my own house!" Those are all good goals! And that's a big purchase, that requires some planning and some intentionality.

Imagine this scenario: you're at work on a Friday, and some friends message you on social media, letting you know they are headed out for a weekend of fun. You're so torn! You love these friends; they're some of your favorite people! But you know how this works; you pop open that handy dandy budget, check your spending for the week/month, review your goals, and *BOOM!* you can make an informed decision about whether or not to go.

Having a working budget can also help you get a good look at your spending habits. Let's say you've been working on your budget for about a year, and you begin to notice some trends. February, for example, seems to be a time you spend lots of money on "household expenses." Why is that? Maybe you're snowed in and bored. Maybe you're longing for spring. Maybe the winter weather is hard on things, and you need to plan better to take care of things during the winter months. Whatever it is, the budget gives you the information you need to begin to see real change in your finances.

Those are some of the things a good budget can do for you. But let's take just a minute and talk about what a budget *won't* do for you.

A budget won't solve your immediate financial problems. In the process of creating your budget, you may have discovered that you have much more money going out than coming in; the budget itself can't fix that. It won't pay your bills, get you a good job, or bail you out of a mess. It can give you the information, but it cannot do it for you.

A budget does not make decisions for you. Once again, the budget is strictly *information.* It is numbers. It does not address the issues in your heart, the ones that call out for that expensive new purse or third vacation. It can help you discover what and where those issues might be, but it will not solve them for you. It will not make decisions for you.

Stewardship is a heart issue, not a numbers issue. Whether or not you are a good steward of the gifts and resources God has given you is up to you.

In my counseling, I have found that many people seem to chafe against creating and sticking to a budget. As we discussed earlier, many of us simply don't want the accountability about our spending! But even if we are willing to make the investment in creating a budget, many people find themselves unable to stick to the plan, and they end up giving up.

Why does this happen? It's very common.

First of all, many people talk about budgeting, and may even create a plan, but they don't make it a priority. What is a priority? The dictionary defines it as something given special, or primary attention. If we let other things take priority over getting control of our budget, we will find ourselves in the same place we've always been.

It takes time and energy to manage a budget well. With time and practice, it becomes easier, but in the early stages it's important to budget not just our money, but the time necessary to properly organize and manage the budget we've created. It takes time to prioritize eating at home rather than eating out. It takes prioritizing the time to write down our spending in our little notebook, to track every little bit so we have a realistic grasp on things, and it's easy to let other things get in the way. In order for a budget to work, it has to be a priority.

Another obstacle to successful budgeting is not understanding how your budget works. There are many budgeting plans and workbooks on the market; you may need to spend some time finding the right tools for you. When you don't understand the tools you're using, you won't use them. Find something that works for you (we have suggestions in the appendix)!

To that end, one reason many budgets fail is because we don't accurately record our spending. We've estimated or guessed at some of the numbers, instead of doing the work to make things accurate. For example, because I didn't record things correctly, I may have overestimated my grocery spending by $30; so, when it comes time to put gas in my car, I don't have the money in the budget. Go back over your Budget Worksheet and make sure you've accurately recorded everything!

One of the main reasons I see budgets fail is because peer pressure is a very real thing. For example, let's use Suzie. Suzie has budgeted $30 per week for entertainment. On Tuesday, Suzie went to hit a bucket of golf balls and have a drink with friends after work, spending her $30. On Friday, her friend Julie calls, and wants to go to the movies. Suzie gives in, because she loves her friend and wants to spend time with her.

Do you see what happened there? Instead of prioritizing her budget, Suzie gave in to the desire to be with friends. Maybe she felt like she had to give in—nobody wants to be seen as the cheapskate, right? Or maybe she was tired, and didn't feel like telling Julie the truth. Either way, she gave up on her budget, and didn't stick to her goals.

"But I like my friends," you say. "I want to hang out with them!" Of course, you do. No one is telling you not to! But instead of spending $30 on dinner and a movie, what if Suzie had been honest with Julie, telling her about her budget priorities and inviting her over for home cooking and game night? If your budget is truly a priority, you will find creative ways to stick to it.

My husband likes to use what we call the "24-Hour Rule." Anytime you're faced with a decision about how to spend money outside of your budget, give it 24 hours. Many times, whether it's a big purchase, a big outing, or something else, just giving it some time will help you maintain your perspective.

Perhaps one beautiful, sunny Saturday afternoon, you decide to do a little car "window" shopping. "Just a test drive," you tell yourself. "Won't that be fun?" So down to the dealer you go, fully intending to drive a fun car, dream a little, and head home for a peanut butter sandwich.

But when you get to the dealer, you happen to meet the Salesman of the Month, Sam, who shows you the *exact* car you've been dreaming about since you got your license, all those many years ago. Color, style, speed—it's all there. And look—satellite radio thrown in for free (for the first three months)! What a deal!

Sam somehow manages to get you into the showroom, and proceeds to ask you, "What do I need to do to get you into this car today?" Sam goes back and forth with the "manager," somehow able to promise everything you've ever wanted.

But wait! You stop, remembering your goals. Your plan. Your budget. Glancing outside, you see your old car. It needs some repairs, your mechanic says. Maybe a few hundred dollars in repairs, even. It'll need new tires in a few months too. Staring down at the contract in front of you, you pause. Margaret's book taught you the "24-Hour Rule," and you know you're still learning about all this budget stuff. She's been right so far, you think, so why wouldn't she be right this time?

You look at Sam, saying, "Thank you, but I need to think about this for a day." You smile, politely sidestepping Sam's growing frustration that you are indeed walking out the door without a signed contract, and without the keys to a brand new car. Keeping your mind set on your priorities, on what God has told you to do, you walk resolutely to your car and get in.

For the next 24 hours, every time you get in your old car you think about that new car. How it smelled, how it sounded when you revved the engine ... and then you think about being debt-free, no car payment hanging over your head for the next few years. Finally, by the end of the 24 hours, you are glad you stood strong and held to your priorities. Go you!!

Ok, that's a pretty dramatic example. But what would it look like if you stood that firmly for your new budgeting priorities, all the time? What if you took a few minutes and prepared your coffee the night before, so you're not tempted to stop at Tim Horton's again on your way to work?

Perhaps Suzie could have solved her problem ahead of time by being honest with Julie about what God was doing in her life. If Julie is really a good friend, she will support Suzie's goals!

One way to overcome these obstacles is by talking about the differences between *needs* and *wants.* In Matthew 6, Jesus says this: *"Therefore I tell you, do not worry about your life, what you will eat or drink; or about your body, what you will wear. Is not life more than food, and the body more than clothes? Look at the birds of the air; they do not sow or reap or store away in barns, and yet your heavenly Father feeds them. Are you not much more valuable than they? Can any one of you by worrying add a single hour to your life?*

"And why do you worry about clothes? See how the flowers of the field grow. They do not labor or spin. Yet I tell you that not even Solomon in all his splendor was dressed like one of these. If that is how God clothes the grass of the field, which is here today and tomorrow is thrown into the fire, will he not much more clothe you— you of little faith? So, do not worry, saying, 'What shall we eat?' or 'What shall we drink?' or 'What shall we wear?' For the pagans run after all these things, and your heavenly Father knows that you need them. But seek first his kingdom and his righteousness, and all these things will be given to you as well. Therefore, do not worry about tomorrow, for tomorrow will worry about itself. Each day has enough trouble of its own" (v. 25-34).

Jesus reminds us here that He has all of our needs well taken care of, and not to worry about them. What does He mean by *need*?

We need food to live, obviously. But we might not *need* steak and lobster, when tuna or a hamburger might do just fine. We need good food, food that will help our bodies work right; but we might not need the exotic smoothie at the shop, when we can make a perfectly good one at home. We need a roof over our heads, and running water and electricity are important. We need clothes to wear.

But many times, we decide that we *need* that fancy new purse, or that new book by our favorite author, or that brand new couch. There's nothing wrong with these things; these are simply *wants.* Sometimes I want a cookie. I never actually *need* a cookie, but sometimes I want one. And then I have to stop and think, how does eating this cookie fit in with my priorities and goals? If I have a goal to lose 20 lbs., and I ate a pile of French fries at lunch, that cookie might not fit. But if I'm on track with my goals, one cookie will actually fit right in.

I've often said I would not purchase another book. I have all these books at home that I need to read and I have all these periodicals coming. I promised the Lord I would not spend money on another book. I went off to a conference and of course, the conference was on writing; they had authors there, and the authors had their books for sale. I could not stick to my promise! For a short time there, I forgot my own priorities! I love conferences, and I love books. It can be difficult to set those things aside when a *really good opportunity* comes up, a conference with some of my favorite speakers or books by my favorite authors. It's helpful to always have my budget accessible, and to frequently remind myself of my goals and priorities.

When building your budget, consider prioritizing needs first, but then consider how you might save for those wants. One person I know has built buying books into her budget. When she has spent that money, she knows she can go to her local library or swap books with a friend if she needs more to read. Another man has decided to put off saving for a new car until he is out of debt.

Look at it this way. You need to get to work, right? An economy car will get you there as well as a luxury vehicle; and if you live in a city where this is possible, public transportation might be a good option as well. Or consider walking or biking during good weather. I frequently find free podcasts by my favorite speakers, and I frequent my local library whenever possible to find good books.

It's not that Jesus doesn't want us to have nice things; quite the contrary! He wants to be sure we remember that He meets all of our needs. And if we'll budget and save and be good stewards, we'll get to have our wants too!

Over the years I have learnt that God takes on a journey that is made to glorify Him. Sometimes the way we view the plan and execution are tweaked by what gives Him the best exposure. Usually the outcome His way is so much better than anything we could ask for. So, if you aren't where you want to be, seek out God. Knock on His door. Ask Him for the desires of your heart and if they are in His will, He will grant them. He loves surprising us by granting us our hearts desire from left field.

HOMEWORK:

1. Make a list of your needs. Make sure you include *everything.*

2. Now make a list of your *wants*. Again, make sure you include everything. It doesn't matter how big or how small—list it!
3. Compare the two lists. Are there wants that belong on the needs list? Are there needs that belong on the wants list?
4. Take these lists to the Lord in prayer. Ask Him to speak to you about meeting your needs. Then take those needs to your Gratitude Journal, and list the ones He's already met!
5. Be honest about your wants list. Submit that to the Lord too. Let Him hear everything—and then let Him speak to you about them. Journal what He says; I think you might be surprised about some things!
6. How are you doing keeping up with your Spending Tracker? By now, you should have a pretty good idea of your spending habits. You should have a pretty solid list of all of your spending categories, and be closely tracking your spending in those areas.

CHAPTER 6 - Dealing with Idols

"No one can serve two masters, for either he will hate the one and love the other, or he will be devoted to the one and despise the other. You cannot serve God and money."
Matthew 6:24

PRAYER: *Lord, today I choose You. I choose You to be my source of truth, my source of comfort, my source of everything. I choose to find my security and my purpose in You and You alone. I know You won't ever let me down! Amen.*

The Gospels of Matthew, Mark and Luke all tell the story of a young man who came to Jesus one day. Luke describes him as a "ruler"; but all three accounts say this man was rich. He came to Jesus, and asked Him, "What do I need to do to be saved?"

Jesus' response is this: *"You know the commandments: 'Do not commit adultery, Do not murder, Do not steal, Do not bear false witness, Honor your father and mother'"* (Luke 18:20). The young man replies that he has kept all these. Jesus then takes it a step further, and says, *"One thing you still lack. Sell all that you have and distribute to the poor, and you will have treasure in heaven; and come, follow me"* (v. 22). Luke then reports that the young man went away sad, because he was very rich.

What was Jesus' point? Was he saying that wealth was bad? Not at all. What Jesus was getting to with this young man is the young man's response: he was so attached to his money that even when faced with eternal life, he couldn't let go. His heart was already taken—by his money.

Timothy Keller, in his book *Counterfeit Gods,* defines this as an *idol,* something that so grips your heart and your mind that it easily becomes your source of happiness, of identity, and of your definition of success. Another term for idol might be "false god," something we worship— and maybe even love.

Matthew 6:21 says, *"For where your treasure is, there your heart will be also."* I think oftentimes we think of this the other way around; where I put my I treasure, I will love. If I treasure material things, wealth, or making money, that is where my heart will be focused.

Several years ago, I was preparing to take the exams to become a Certified Accountant. I had worked so hard for this, had spent years in a classroom and years studying. In the days and weeks leading up to the exams, I could think of nothing else; becoming a CPA was the answer to all my problems, I knew. If I could just pass the test and get my certification, everything would finally fall into place, and I would be happy. I just knew it!

It felt like my life fell apart when I didn't pass the first time. For days, I felt like nothing was worth living for, that I was a failure. My career goals had become an idol in my life. They had begun to speak to me about my value and worth, and my heart was broken when that idol didn't come through for me.

Because you see, idols can never come through for us. They can never fulfill us, or provide a true source of happiness or identity. They're not meant to. We are meant to find our source of happiness and fulfillment in God alone; anything else, anywhere else we go to get those needs met, is an idol.

What are some areas of idolatry?

One of the most common areas of idolatry is *materialism,* the constant pursuit of *things.* This could look like always wanting a bigger, fancier house, or a faster, flashier car. It could look like having a closet stuffed full of clothes you can't afford, and that maybe you never wear; you just have to *have* the clothes. Most of the time, it's not even really a question of whether or not you can afford things. I know plenty of people who are consumed with things, no matter what their financial situation is.

The dictionary defines materialism as, "preoccupation with or emphasis on material objects, comforts, and considerations, with a disinterest in or rejection of spiritual, intellectual, or cultural values."

In our culture, we've seen the rise of a strange phenomenon. We have the ability to buy larger and larger homes, with ample storage space—and yet there's been a boon of storage rental facilities. For all of the space we can buy, we still can't fit all of our stuff in it. Why is that? I suspect it's because many of us have actually bought into the lie of materialism, that somehow more stuff will equal greater status, or more meaningful lives, or more happiness. And what does this emphasis on stuff get us? A monthly charge to store things we never use, perhaps, and if we can store them in our own houses, more to clean and care for!

Materialism leads to another idol—comparison. "Well, so-and-so just bought a bigger house! I'm so jealous—maybe if I had that house, then I would be happy!" I know that sounds funny; of course, you and I have never actually had that thought, right? Of course not. But maybe we've had the feeling attached to it, that somehow because someone has a bigger house, or a nicer car, or more money, or whatever, that they must somehow be happier than we are. Or a more dangerous thought—that God must love them more than He loves us.

In our cultural pursuit of materialism, we've somehow come to equate God's favor with *things.* That somehow, He's only a good father if we have nice stuff or a full bank account. But nowhere—nowhere—in the Bible does it describe God as this kind of father at all! Bill Johnson says that "Jesus is perfect theology;" in other words, if we want to know what God is like, we just need to look at Jesus. Well, did Jesus have a bunch of stuff that He dragged around Israel with Him? No, of course not. But yet we know that God said Jesus was His Son, in whom He (God the Father) was well-pleased. So, to equate material things with favor is to call Jesus un-favored.

Doesn't make any sense, does it? Of course not. But yet sometimes we feel those feelings of jealousy when someone else prospers, don't we? We compare our success to others. One of the most dangerous effects of this idol is that if we base our success as compared to others, then we are constantly hoping for others to fail. I know that sounds harsh, but think about it: if I am threatened by others' success, then I need them to actually fail so that I can consider myself successful. How am I supposed to live in relationship and community with people if I am constantly hoping for their demise?

There's one root for these idols, and for others too: a spirit of poverty. A spirit of poverty believes that there will never be enough, that God isn't a good provider, that He is not a good Father, and that I have to work my fingers to the bone for everything I have. Notice that a spirit of poverty has nothing to do with how much money you actually have; it's a mindset, a way of looking at the world. I know people with a spirit of poverty who have more money in their bank account than I will ever see in my life, and I know people who have next to nothing in their bank account, but do not have this spirit.

A spirit of poverty manifests itself in greed, in never having enough. That could mean never having enough money, never having enough food, never having enough things—just never enough. And as we described earlier, closely related to greed is jealousy, constantly comparing what I have to what others have. (This could also be about someone else's fitness, or marriage, or friendships. It's not just about money.) It may feel confrontational to call it that, but that's just what it is.

How do you know if you are operating with this spirit?

One way to know if something is an idol is to examine what you daydream about. What occupies your mind when you have nothing else to think about? Is it a new car? A new job? Is it more clothes, or maybe the new outfit you saw someone else wearing that you just have to have? Maybe it's this year's vacation. Or think of it this way: what do you habitually think about to get joy and comfort in the privacy of your own heart?

Where do you go for comfort? For joy? For peace? For significance? If your answer is anything other than God, those things have become idols in your heart.

Where do you spend your money? If it's true that where your treasure is, your heart will be, then go back and take a look at your spending. Your money flows most effortlessly toward your heart's greatest love. The mark of an idol is that you spend too much money on it, to the detriment of other things. Do you frequently shop for clothes—and then have to skimp on groceries or other bills? Is your car payment more than your house payment? Are you taking vacations that put you into debt? These are signs of idols, and of operating under a spirit of poverty.

Ultimately, a spirit of poverty is rooted in unbelief: unbelief that God is good, that He loves me, and that He will provide what I need. 2 Kings tells the story of Naaman, a commander of the army of the King of Syria. Naaman was what the Bible calls a "man of valor," but he also had leprosy, which in those days was incurable. An Israeli girl was working in his house, and told Naaman's wife that if Naaman were only in Israel, the prophet (Elisha) could cure him of the disease.

Naaman went to the king of Syria, who wrote a letter to the king of Israel. Elisha found out about it, and told the king to let Naaman come to him.

So Naaman showed up at Elisha's house, with horses and chariots—with his wealth and influence on full display. He wanted to be sure that Elisha knew exactly who he was. But instead of coming out himself, Elisha sent a messenger, telling Naaman to go wash in the Jordan River seven times, and he would be healed.

But this wasn't good enough for Naaman. He got angry. He thought that because of his wealth and power, that Elisha would come out himself and just wave his hand around, and then Naaman would be healed. He yelled about the rivers in his home country of Syria being "better" than the rivers in Israel.

Can you just hear the materialism and the comparison and the pride?

Naaman really thought that he could somehow buy favor with the prophet, and when he couldn't, the spirit of poverty manifested in anger and defensiveness. "How dare he! Doesn't he know who I am?"

Have you ever thought that? If that person just knew who you were, how much money you had, how much influence, what job you had, who you were married to, etc., then they wouldn't treat you that way! They would give you that job, or that money, or whatever. But even that sense of entitlement is a sign of a spirit of poverty at work. It's the overwhelming sense that God won't come through for me, and I have to do it myself.

Back to Naaman. One of his servants came to him and basically said, "Why not do it? You wanted a word from the prophet, and you got it. Why not go wash?" Naaman must have calmed down, because he went and washed in the Jordan, just as Elisha had said. And lo and behold, he was healed!

How many times have we been angry with God, because it looked like He didn't "come through" for us? Or how many times have we been worried and anxious, stressing about this thing or that? But if we'll just obey what He's already told us to do, we'll find ourselves healed, whole, and provided for.

What Jesus was offering that rich young man was far more valuable than whatever wealth the young man had. But the young man was operating in a spirit of poverty, despite being wealthy. He didn't understand that his riches and wealth would pass away, but eternal life is— well, eternal.

Mark 8:36 says, *"What good is it for someone to gain the whole world, yet forfeit their soul?"* In other words, what are you willing to exchange for eternal life? Like that rich young man, what idols are you hanging onto that are keeping you from the freedom and life that Jesus has for you? Isn't it time to let them go?

HOMEWORK:

Here's an exercise for you. Imagine that you are the rich young ruler, and Jesus asks you to give up everything and follow Him. Could you do it? Why or why not?

What things are you hanging onto? Allow Jesus to speak to the areas where you may have idols. Is it things? Is it your bank account?

Two of the major areas in which we tend to have idols are comparison and pride. Do you often compare your situation to others? Do you find yourself feeling frustrated when others succeed?

Or do you find yourself feeling more important than others because of your position or financial status? Take some time this week and examine your heart in these areas. Allow the Lord to speak to those things, and then be prepared to tear down those idols!!

Pray: *Lord, today I choose to set aside anything I've used as a source of security or self-worth. I realize that my value comes from You and You alone. It doesn't matter what anyone else has or what anyone else does!*

Lord, are there any areas in which I've created idols? (Listen for His response!) *I confess that I've put those things in Your place, God. Today I choose to tear them down!*

Lord, would You show me what it would look like for You to be my source? (Let Him speak! Then journal what He shows you.)

Secondly, you may have recognized in yourself evidence of a spirit of poverty. Take some time and pray this:

Lord, I repent of any way that I've agreed with a spirit of poverty. You are not a God of lack; You are a God of abundance! You are not holding out on me. You are not holding back. You have only good things in store for me, and today I choose to agree with that!

You may need to pray that every day this week, or even more than once a day. Begin to recognize ways in which you've been living from a place of poverty rather than abundance. Your good Father has only good things in store for you!

CHAPTER 7 - Coping with Difficult Times

And my God will supply every need of yours
according to his riches in glory in Christ Jesus.
Philippians 4:19

PRAYER: *Lord, sometimes things are hard. I have situations in my life where I need You. Badly. Would You come and talk to me about those things? I need Your wisdom. I need Your provision. I need Your presence. Amen.*

"I observed a stately lion resting in the afternoon sun. That lion's long tail was in constant motion wagging back and forth, back and forth, trying to keep a nagging swarm of flies at bay. Even the king of the jungle has to fight flies."

Deanna sat uncomfortably in what would normally be her most comfortable chair. Her mind raced as she mindlessly tapped her pencil on the pad of paper in front of her. She glanced down; the paper was covered in columns of numbers, written, calculated, crossed out.

The bills had been piling up for a little while, but she hadn't worried too much about it—until Jim lost his job. It seemed so unfair after all the years of faithful service he had given the company! And even though Jim was now drawing unemployment, it was not enough to make ends meet. On top of everything else, the doctor had confirmed that their son Shawn needed surgery. It couldn't be postponed without putting Shawn in danger, and now there was no insurance to cover it. The medical costs would be astronomical.

Deanna looked at the numbers again, adding the amount in the savings account to the checking account and then subtracting the monthly bills. It still didn't add up. She went through each possible solution; when none presented itself, she burst into tears.

This scenario is all too common in our pressured lives. Medical problems, job loss, divorce, or other things that drain finances provide the ingredients for stress and anxiety in the lives of many, many people. When we haven't prepared, and even sometimes when we have, times get tough. Most of us will go through times like this, at one point or another.

So, what do we do about it?

In Numbers 13, Moses sent one man from each tribe, including Joshua and Caleb, to spy out the land of Canaan. Verse 17-20 says, *"Moses sent them to spy out the land of Canaan and said to them, "Go up into the Negeb and go up into the hill country, and see what the land is, and whether the people who dwell in it are strong or weak, whether they are few or many, and whether the land that they dwell in is good or bad, and whether the cities that they dwell in are camps or strongholds, and whether the land is rich or poor, and whether there are trees in it or not. Be of good courage and bring some of the fruit of the land."*

Remember, this was the Promised Land! This was the hope God had placed before them; now they were standing in front of it, and Moses wanted to know what awaited them once they got there. So, he sent the group of men to spy, to report back what they found.

Beginning in verse 25: *"At the end of forty days they returned from spying out the land. And they came to Moses and Aaron and to all the congregation of the people of Israel in the wilderness of Paran, at Kadesh. They brought back word to them and to all the congregation, and showed them the fruit of the land. And they told him, "We came to the land to which you sent us. It flows with milk and honey, and this is its fruit. However, the people who dwell in the land are strong, and the cities are fortified and very large. And besides, we saw the descendants of Anak there. The Amalekites dwell in the land of the Negeb. The Hittites, the Jebusites, and the Amorites dwell in the hill country. And the Canaanites dwell by the sea, and along the Jordan""* (v. 25-29).

Giants! They had seen giants in the land! "It flows with milk and honey," they said, and presented Moses with grapes, an example of the fruit growing there. But there were giants awaiting them! How would they ever possess the Promised Land with those giants in the way?

You've probably faced some giants, maybe even since beginning this process of aiming for financial freedom. You know that you know that God spoke to you, and that He's prepared a Promised Land in the area of your finances. So, you've begun to "spy out the land," so to speak, and it just looks impossible.

Or maybe you've been doing just fine—and then the diagnosis. Or the layoff. Or the sudden divorce. Something rears its ugly head between you and living in the Promised Land. Like Deanna, the numbers just don't add up. You don't know where the money is going to come from, and things look pretty bleak.

What do you do?

Going back to our band of merry men, we can look at two different responses. One group, the majority actually, gave the report above. Yes, the land is rich, and yes, the land it fruitful. But no, we can't possess it; too many enemies! Too many giants!

Often when we talk about money, the "giants" look like this: too many bills and obligations, and not enough income. These can certainly be obstacles, and can seem insurmountable. But many times, the giants don't have dollar signs attached to them.

Instead, the biggest roadblocks in our lives look more like bitterness, doubt, discouragement, infirmity, jealousy, or disobedience. And all of these giants are rooted in one big one: *fear.*

Why do so many people remain in debt, enslaved to jobs they hate, unable to do the things they really want to do? Why do people continue living paycheck to paycheck, barely scraping by? I think it's because they're afraid.

Afraid of what??

The reason most people don't do well on diets isn't because they don't know what they should and shouldn't eat or that they should exercise. Most diets fail because people feel *deprived.* The instant they start thinking about what they *can't have,* that thing is all they can think about. Have you ever decided to go on a diet? I can almost bet that the very next morning, all you could think about is all the things you couldn't have.

It's the same with budgeting. Many people think that if they really start sticking to a budget, they'll have to give up everything fun. Or at least that's what it feels like. Budgeting, saving—these things feel restricting! We want our freedom!

Or so we think. Proverbs 29:18 says, *"Where there is no revelation, people cast off restraint; but blessed is the one who heeds wisdom's instruction."* Revelation of what?

Revelation of God's goodness, His nearness, and His heart toward us. His heart isn't that we would live enslaved to our finances, to anxiety, to worry. His heart is that we would experience the freedom that "wisdom's instruction" brings. What would it look like if you lived in such a way that you could pay all of your bills, have plenty to eat and drink and wear, give to your church and other charities as you like, and occasionally go on a nice, relaxing vacation with your family? This is what "wisdom's instruction" will provide for you ... provided you listen.

Ever since Genesis 3, mankind has been in the business of taking care of him or herself. The problem in Genesis 3 is not that Adam and Eve ate a piece of fruit they weren't supposed to eat; the problem in Genesis 3 is that once they ate that fruit, they became their own source of identity, of wisdom, of provision. They stopped looking to God to meet all of their needs—as He had done from the day He created them—and started to decide to meet their own needs, their own way.

We've been living this way ever since.

The book of Proverbs refers to "wisdom" as a person, someone who "calls out" to travelers on the road. "Wisdom" would cry out to us to not get into that crazy debt, to not spend that money we don't have, to not look to what we can buy as our source of identity and purpose; instead, "wisdom" would cry out to us to get to know Jehovah Jireh—our Provider. (Genesis 22:14)

God desires to provide for us. He loves to take care of His children! As we discussed earlier, God is a good, good Father, who desires to give "all good gifts" to His children.

I know that, you say. Of course you do. We all know that—in our heads. We can recite the right words, sing the right songs, probably even quote chapter and verse. But yet our consumption of sleep aids and antacids might prove otherwise. If we really know how good God is, and that His desire is to provide for us, why are we still so stressed? Why, when faced with our giants in the land, do we respond like the other men? Why don't we respond like Caleb, with faith and hope, even when we really want to?

There is a biblical and spiritual principle that would say, "You become what you focus on." In other words, your thoughts matter. Your focus matters. What you say to yourself matters. What you rehearse becomes your reality. Consider these verses:

Colossians 3:2 *"Set your minds on things on things above, not on earthly things."*

Matthew 6:33 *"But seek first his kingdom and his righteousness, and all these things will be given to you as well."*

Romans 8:5-7 *"Those who live according to the flesh have their minds set on what the flesh desires; but those who live in accordance with the Spirit have their minds set on what the Spirit desires. The mind governed by the flesh is death, but the mind governed by the Spirit is life and peace. The mind governed by the flesh is hostile to God; it does not submit to God's law, nor can it do so."*

The verses from Romans teach us a very important principle, that we have power over our minds! Look at verse 5: *"Those who live according to the flesh **have their minds set** on what the flesh desires; but those who live in accordance with the Spirit **have their minds set** on what the Spirit desires"* (emphasis mine). Paul is telling us here that we can actually choose what we set our minds on! We have a choice! In His brilliance, God gave us a will, and we can use it!

The rest of the passage from Romans gives us a glimpse into what the result of our choice looks like: death, or life and peace. Does that sound familiar? When you focus on what God is doing, on who He is, on His nature, His character, His Word, you can feel the life and peace flowing. When you choose to set your mind elsewhere— well, I probably don't have to tell you what that feels like.

This is why the Gratitude Journal is so important! The purpose of this journal is to help us learn to rehearse what God is already doing in our lives. He's always up to something, and practicing gratefulness *sets our minds* on Him.

Consider Deanna, from our story at the beginning of this chapter. By going over the numbers again and again and again, she was practicing over and over how bad things were. She was rehearsing her lack, and what seemed like it could never work out.

But should she deny her problems, you ask? Of course not. Deanna and Jim's situation was very real, and very difficult. In the movie "Bridge of Spies" with Tom Hanks, a character is arrested for spying on the United States.

James Donovan (Tom Hanks): I have a mandate to serve you. Nobody else does. Quite frankly, everybody else has an interest in sending you to the electric chair.

Rudolf Abel: All right ...

James Donovan: You don't seem alarmed.

Rudolf Abel: Would it help?

Abel's refrain of "Would it help?" is repeated throughout the movie, every time someone asks him if he's worried about things over which he has no control. Of course, it wouldn't help; Abel knows that, and so do we.

But we do it anyway, as if worrying by itself can change our situation! So instead of worrying, let me introduce you to a concept.

Don't freak out: I'm about to talk to you about Biblical meditation. Most believers would probably define "meditation" as something those hippies do with their eastern guru, sitting cross-legged and glassy-eyed, repeating some random sound over and over. I suppose this is a kind of meditation, asking you to clear your mind of all thoughts except this sound or whatever.

Biblical meditation still involves the mind, but instead of being a passive thing, it's quite active and intentional. The intent of biblical meditation isn't to help someone escape from their circumstances; rather, the purpose of meditation is to strengthen your faith, to strengthen your connection with the Lord, to "set your mind" on things of God. It is very strategically renewing your mind—something we are commanded to do in Romans 12:2: *"Do not conform to the pattern of this world, but be transformed by the renewing of your mind."*

So how do we do this? You can compare the idea of biblical meditation to that of a cow chewing its cud (I know; stay with me here). A cow eats grass. The chewed-up grass goes into one of the cow's stomachs, then gets regurgitated so the cow can chew on it again before swallowing it. Biblical meditation looks something like this. We take a verse (I'll give you some suggestions for homework), and continue to chew on it over hours or days or even weeks, bringing it up in our prayers, our thoughts, our journaling, over and over. By doing this, we "chew and swallow" God's word, getting it deep into our minds and hearts.

This is something we practice; it may not come easy. But when we face situations like Jim and Deanna, how much would it help us to be able to recall those Scriptures, to bring them to mind one more time? To be able to choose our focus?

This *discipline*, or practice, of memorizing and meditating on the Word brings up another point. Very often when our situation looks impossible, it's actually not impossible; remember we serve a God with whom all things are possible! But often in our anxiety and worry, we are not able to see a clear path through to the other side. The practice of biblical meditation teaches us how to get our minds off of our circumstances, and onto the Lord.

When we do that, that seems to be the time when "wisdom" shows up. By meditating and focusing on Him and His Word, we become perfectly positioned for Him to show us exactly what we need to do to face our situation!

Once He's shown us what to do, then the next principle kicks in: the discipline to follow through. You see, many times the Lord will miraculously deliver us from our circumstances (that is in effect what Jesus did on the Cross!); but other times, He will give us a very clear path—and ask us to choose to stick to it.

This requires discipline. Maybe you're like me, and the word "discipline" brings up memories of being spanked or getting grounded to your room. But the word can also mean "to train by instruction and exercise; drill; to bring a state of order and obedience by training and control." In other words, discipline is a choice to bring order into your life by intention—on purpose.

God will give you strategies to get through your circumstances, but He will not force you to do those things. God is not a puppet master, pulling our strings; He has given us the choice whether or not we obey. And many times, His strategies involve restraint or boundaries around one area, so that we can experience true freedom in another area. It's not easy. Remember this, though: every time you say "yes" to one thing, you are saying "no" to another.

When you say "yes" to that sweater you can't really afford, you are saying "no" to the new car you are saving up for. When you say "yes" to that expensive night out with your friends, you are saying "no" to getting out of debt that much sooner.

Discipline requires focus. It requires knowing why we do what we do, and being confident in just Who has given us those strategies. This is especially important when we are faced with difficult circumstances, as it's easy to lose our focus. Remember the lion from the quote at the beginning of this chapter? Even the king of the jungle has to swat at flies. Everyone has difficult times. Everyone.

Keep your plan always in front of you. Remind yourself daily why you are doing what you are doing. Practice the rewards coming, if you'll stick to it: debt free, prepared for the future, ability to pay bills, newer car (no payment!!), etc. Rehearse it! Remind yourself. That's why earlier in the book, we wrote out our goals and put them in a place where we can see them all the time.

Don't lose focus when things go wrong. Consider Caleb, and his response to what others saw as "giants": Caleb knew the Promised Land was theirs. He knew who their God was, what God had told them to do—and He knew that if they would just obey, they could go in and possess the land!

HOMEWORK:

1. In this chapter, I listed some verses to meditate on. Go back and pick one, and spend time this week meditating as described in the chapter. Don't worry about studying the verse, or translating it, or anything else. Simply meditate on it.
2. Proverbs 21:20 says, *"The wise store up choice food and olive oil, but fools gulp theirs down."* In other words, wise people have a plan. They store and save—for any situation.

Do you have a plan for an emergency? Or like Deanna, would you be thrown off completely by a sudden emergency?

Having an Emergency Fund is something most people don't think about— until they need it. They don't think about it until the car accident, the appliance meltdown, or the catastrophic illness. Those things are likely to happen to any of us at any time; according to Proverbs, it is wise for us to be prepared for such things!

Go to your Spending Tracker and your budget. You're going to create a new item:

"Emergency Fund." Begin to set aside an amount from every paycheck, even if it's just a few dollars. Perhaps you can go without a latte a couple of times a week so that you can begin to create your Emergency Fund!

Some people create another bank account for this fund, so that they don't spend it on other things. Others set aside a place where they set aside cash: maybe a bureau drawer or a home safe or something like that. Decide what would work best for you, and begin putting money aside. You will be wise to do so!

CHAPTER 8 - Setting Goals

*"Before they call I will answer; while they
are yet speaking I will hear."*
Isaiah 65:24

PRAYER: *Lord, I know You hear me when I call. I know You
are intimately acquainted with all my ways! Thank You for
being a good Father, for loving me so much! Today I choose
to submit my plans to you, God. Be my guide, be my wise
counselor. Lead me and guide me! Amen.*

If you've ever flown on an airplane, you probably don't
think much about the planning that goes into how you
get from the point of departure to the destination. You
simply buy your ticket, pack your swimsuit, and get on
the plane. And unless there's bad weather or some other
unusual event, within a few hours, you arrive just where
you intended to arrive.

The reality is, the pilot and co-pilot have done hours and
years of preparation for your plane ride. They have
trained, studied, spent hours in a simulator, and the day
of your flight, they have filed what's known as a "flight
plan" for that particular flight. A flight plan describes the
precise route the airplane will take to reach its
destination. It must be precise; even a mistake of one
small degree can send the plane to an entirely different
destination.

You could say that the "flight plan" serves as a goal for
the pilots. They may take off from New York City, and the
goal is to land in Los Angeles. Every decision they make,

every knob they turn and button they push gets them to their destination.

As you set and implement your budget, keep this principle in mind. What is your goal? You can set a budget, but if you haven't yet filed your flight plan, you might not be sure of your "why." *Why* do you need a budget? What is your purpose for gaining control of your finances? What's your *destination?*

Take some time this week and consider your *why.* Why are you working on your budget? Why are you taking the time and energy to dig into your spending and saving habits? *Why?* It's time to talk about setting some goals.

For our purposes, we are going to discuss two kinds of goals in this chapter. *Financial goals,* and *faith goals.* It may seem like these two things aren't related to one another, but I think you'll find, as I have, that they are much more closely tied to each other than we might think.

Financial goals, in the general sense, often look like this: increase income, and decrease spending. Balance the budget. Or, in some cases, actually *create* a budget. Then we may have more specific goals: save for a house or a car. Pay for kids' college. Increase giving.

Your *why* may look different than someone else's. Let's look at some possibilities.

Perhaps you want to own a home. Perhaps you would like to be able to send your children to college. Perhaps you have old debt you would like to be rid of. Perhaps you want to leave your children a legacy of financial health. Or perhaps you have simply been convicted about being a good steward of what God has given you, and you know you have some work to do.

Having your reasons always in front of you will help you set your goals. If you've gotten this far in the book, I assume you already have a *why;* if not, go ahead and skip to this week's homework, then come back and finish reading the chapter.

Once you have discovered your why, it's time to set some goals.

This method of goal-setting can be used for any goals you'd like to set: financial goals, weight loss or fitness goals, time management goals, project goals ... the list goes on. We are going to use what is called the SMART method. SMART stands for **s**pecific, **m**easurable, **a**ttainable, **r**ealistic, and **t**imely. We are going to look at each one of these individually.

Specific – make the goal specific. Detailed. What *exactly* do you want to accomplish? It could be you'd like to start tithing. This is specific goal!

Measurable – There is a gauge, a scale, something you can measure. If your goal is to tithe, and you consider 10% of your income the tithe, then you can measure your giving as a percentage of your income. Every month you can apply a very simple math problem to see if you're on track.

Attainable – How realistic is your goal? If you are already maxed out as far as your bills and outgoing money each month, and you've already done everything you can do to reduce spending, you may need to set a different goal of increasing your income before you can work on this goal. But if you are ready, you can set your goal at 10% and begin working toward it!

Realistic – Is my goal realistic? If I set this goal, will I actually do what's necessary to achieve it?

This part requires some thought. I know myself; if I set a goal of running five miles a day, I'm not likely to follow through. I don't like to run. I have bad knees. I don't live in a safe neighborhood, and because I'm reducing my spending, I canceled my gym membership. Nothing about my life would show that I can realistically reach this goal.

If my goal is to tithe 10%, I need to be realistic. Am I committed to a local church body? If not, is there a ministry where I could send my tithe?

Will I actually stick to it? In reality, I'm the only one who knows the answer to this question. Am I committed to being faithful with my tithe? Be realistic with yourself. Perhaps part of working out a goal would be to set smaller goals along the way. I will commit to a 2% tithe. Or a 5% tithe. If I start a little smaller, it might be a bit more realistic—and I might actually follow through!

Timely – Give yourself a deadline. For many people, having a target date helps keep them on track with their goals. "I would like to be tithing 10% at this time next year." Mark it in your calendar. Every month, remind yourself of your approaching deadline.

Let's take a look at this from another perspective. Perhaps in examining your budget and setting your goals, you've figured out that you need to bring in some more income. As you consider this, you remember that time your friend took you to coffee to present a business opportunity that seems like it might work for you: selling Mary Kay cosmetics.

In doing your budget calculations, you figure out that you need about $200 extra a month to make ends meet. One bottle of body wash costs $20, so you need 20 people to buy a bottle of body wash every month. Everybody showers, hopefully every day, so they are most likely going to use up a bottle a month.

Let's put this in terms of our SMART method.

Is it **specific**? Yes. You need 20 people to buy a bottle of body wash every month.

Is it **measurable**? Yes. You'll know if you sold 20 bottles of body wash.

You can take this step further. If you're going to sell 20 bottles, you need actual people to buy them. In thinking about it, you realize you have a rather large family (some of whom might need some extra body wash) and you can start with them. And you have some friends who like to shower, so they are possible customers as well. So you sit down and make a list of all the friends and family members who could potentially buy body wash, and you gather their contact information. You set a **measurable** goal to contact them all in the span of one week.

If your list only includes 18 friends and family members, you know you need to find ways to reach out to at least 2 more people. Or at the end of the week, you've only got 8 friends and family members who agree to buy body wash from you; because you've set a measurable goal of 20, you know you need to get 12 more customers.

Is it **attainable**? You set a goal to get 20 customers by the end of the month. With your schedule and pace of life, making enough connections to meet that goal seems attainable.

Is it **realistic**? This seems pretty close to *attainable*; there is a slight difference. *Is it attainable* asks you if you *can* meet the goal; *is it realistic* asks you if you actually will do the things necessary to meet it. Realistically, if you spend all day on the phone for your telemarketer job, you're not likely to want to spend more time on the phone when you get home. If you spend your evenings running kids around to sports practices and musical rehearsals, you may not have time to make a bunch of phone calls.

Or if all of your friends suddenly decide to stop taking showers, they might not buy body wash from you. (I hope that doesn't happen, for your sake.)

On the other hand, perhaps you have one evening a week you could devote to making the necessary connections. You recognize the value of social media to help you with that, and you know how to leverage that platform in a helpful way. You know exactly which family members to call, and which friends would love to buy from you. You're excited about putting in the work to see this happen, and you know you will follow through. This is what makes a goal *realistic.*

If you know you won't do the things necessary to meet your goal, or you find at the end of the first week that you just don't have the time you thought you did, it's time to revisit the goal and adjust it accordingly.

Finally, is it **timely**? You know you need to sell 20 bottles of body wash per month, and you need it to start this month. So, by the end of the current month, you need to meet your goal. If you get to the 15th of the month and you've only sold 2 bottles, you know you have some work to do before the end of the month!

Using the **SMART** method helps us stay on track and meet our goals. This method can work for any goal you'd like to set; if at any point you find that one of these areas isn't working, you can always adjust it. And if you are not meeting your goal, you can look back at each of these areas to discover where the problem lies—and then adjust it. You may find that using this method helps you discover that you need some different goals altogether!

Once you've set your SMART goal (your *"why"*), now you need to lay out the steps you're going to take to see it happen (your *"how"*).

How are you going to meet your goal? Let's stick with Mary Kay for the moment, and keep things simple. Your steps might look like this:

1. You need to be a Mary Kay rep to sell Mary Kay. So your first order of business is to sign up. Do you know a consultant who can help you get started?

If not, you can look at the Mary Kay website to figure out how to sign up.

2. Is there a startup cost to be a consultant? If so, add that to your list of steps, and set a date: next Friday's payday, for example.

3. You need actual bottles of Mary Kay body wash to sell. Where are you going to get those? If you signed up with a consultant, they can help you with that.

4. Now for your list. Which family members can you contact? What friends could you call? As you make your list, add contact information for each person.

Write out these steps. Make a chart, with a column for the step, the date, and then add a column for the date your complete the step. After each step, write your target date (*timely*). For example, by this Tuesday you are going to contact someone to become a consultant (write down the date). Set a date to buy your starter kit. Then by the following Friday, you will have inventory or know how to get your inventory (write down that date).

Now that you've written out your steps, you're going to look at obstacles. There are two types of obstacles, *perceived* obstacles and real obstacles. These are barriers to achieving your goal, and some of them are real—and some are only real in your head. Let's talk about it.

You may be facing very real obstacles, such as finding the time to put in the work to build a business, or coming up with the money to buy a starter kit. You may not actually know 20 people. These are real obstacles to meeting your goals.

If your obstacle is time, you may need to sit down with your calendar and set some priorities. We will make time for what we see as a priority, and this is no different. You may need to say no to some social engagements, or pop open your computer while you're watching TV after work. Or you may need to get up early on a Saturday to make time for the phone calls or meetings you need to have; but this barrier can be overcome.

If your barrier is money, you may need to ask a friend or relative for a short-term loan. Or you may need to save up for a couple of months in order to have the initial cash to make your business dreams come to life.

Many of us use time and money as an excuse to not take the next step. The reality is, if these steps are a priority for you, you will make the necessary changes.

There is another kind of barrier, though. These kinds of obstacles can feel very, very real, and often are the ones that shut us down and keep us from reaching our goals. These speed bumps sneak up on us, and often we can't even really identify exactly what they are; they're just— there. Slowing us down, keeping us from achieving what we set out to do.

Like—fear. I don't mean fear of the boogey man, or fear of monsters under the bed. I'm referring to things like fear of rejection. Fear of failure. Fear of—success.

What if no one will buy from me? What if they think it's a bad idea? What if I buy a bunch of stuff—and it sits in my garage? What if I buy the starter kit, and I'm stuck with a bunch of product I don't like? *What if I fail?*

Most often, we're not afraid of things like scary movies and monsters. We are afraid of being rejected, of not being enough. And taking on a new business, spending the money, contacting people—what if it doesn't work? These thoughts can be crippling. They can whisper to me, even as I'm making my lists and contacting people: *"This isn't going to work,"* these thoughts say. *"No one will buy from you. Don't risk it! Don't put yourself out there! Stay safe, even if it means not having that extra money."* You know you've had those kinds of thoughts. We all have.

And many times, we listen to them. We allow our fears of what "might" happen to make sure that nothing ever happens. In the Disney Pixar movie "Finding Nemo," Nemo's father has this conversation:

Marlin: I promised I'd never let anything happen to him.

Dory: Hmm. That's a funny thing to promise.

Marlin: What?

Dory: Well, you can't never let anything happen to him. Then nothing would ever happen to him.

Very often, we've had these thoughts for so long about many things, and we're very familiar with them. In fact, we may have grown comfortable with these thoughts. Consequently, we haven't failed at much.

But we haven't succeeded either.

The truth is, some people will not buy your body wash, or lipstick, or insurance, or whatever you're selling. Some people will not use your cleaning service, or babysitting

82

service, or auto repair shop. They just won't, and that's real. That's true. But in all likelihood, it has nothing to do with whether or not they like you, or whether or not you're good at your job. It's simply because they may not want lipstick or babysitting, and they already have good insurance.

That is not about you.

In the Mary Kay training, there's an odd step: "work for your first hundred no's." Why would I work for "no's," you might ask? Once you've had that many people say no to you, you will have begun to realize that *it is not personal.* And by the time you've given your sales pitch to that many people, you've likely perfected it! And—in that hundred no's, you will have gotten some yes's.

Success involves risk. If you aren't failing at anything, you're likely not succeeding at much either. As you move through your goal setting, keep this thought in mind: *What if I succeed?* What if this actually works? What if I make that money I need? And bravely take the first step.

Money—there is always money out there. Money to be made. It will take work, and it will take risk. The Bible is full of people who stepped out despite the obstacles, and were fruitful. You can be too.

HOMEWORK:

1. This week, you're going to nail down your *why.*
   Why are you on this journey of getting your
   finances in order, of budgeting, of learning how to
   be a good steward? Is it for your children? Are you
   ready to be a homeowner? Do you need a new

car? Do you have dreams of traveling? Take some time and journal about your *why*. Keep that *why* in front of you as you go through the rest of this week's homework.

2. Do you have a goal? What is your goal? In your journal, write out your **SMART** process.

3. Finally this week, take some time and examine your fears. What is holding you back from succeeding? In what ways are you sabotaging your own success? Ask the Lord to speak to you about those things. Journal what He says.

CHAPTER 9 - Setting Faith Goals

"Commit to the Lord whatever you do, and he will establish your plans."
Proverbs 16:3

PRAYER: *Lord, I want to know You. I want to be close to You. I want to walk with You, all the days of my life. Teach me how to get to know You more and more! Come close to me, God. Be near. Amen.*

We've talked about financial goals, and of course those are important. But even before we set our financial goals, it's important to set some faith goals.

How can I set faith goals, you might ask? That's a great question!

First and foremost, your faith is birthed out of a place of relationship. Our primary goal as Christians should be to grow ever closer to Jesus, through anything that we do— including through our financial situation.

So how do we set faith goals, if faith is about relationship? Consider any relationship you have. Does that relationship just happen accidentally, or does it take some intentional work? If the relationship—whatever it is, whether a marriage or a friendship or a work relationship or a parent/child relationship—is going to be healthy, it's going to require some intention on the part of both parties.

Primary to growing a healthy relationship is simply spending time together. If you wanted to grow a friendship, you need to spend time together; it's the same with Jesus.

How do I spend time with Him, you might ask? That's another great question!

The answer is simple: prayer. Most often, we think of prayer as bringing Jesus our list of needs, rattling them off at him, and then moving on with our day. But prayer is meant to be much more than that. It's meant to be a give and take, a back and forth—with Him doing much more of the talking than we do. What would it look like for us to approach our prayer life that way? That instead of bringing Him my grocery list of wants and needs, that I come to Him to listen?

Or even more so, just to be with Him? What if we were to approach prayer with the mindset that I'm simply there to spend time in His presence? My husband and I can often just enjoy each other's presence, without saying much of anything at all. Is it possible that our prayer life can look more like that?

And of course we can ask God for anything! Jesus said in John 14:14, *"You may ask me for anything in my name, and I will do it."* He loves to meet our needs! Remember, God is a good Father, and Jesus is One with the Father. They are generous and kind, and we are free to ask them for whatever we need.

This story from a doctor who served in Africa perfectly illustrates this point.

One night I had worked hard to help a mother in labor. But in spite of all we could do, she died, leaving us with a tiny, premature baby and her crying two-year-old daughter. We would have difficulty keeping the baby alive, as we had no incubator. We had no electricity to run an incubator. We also had no special feeding facilities. Although we lived on the equator, nights were often chilly with treacherous drafts.

One student went for the box for such cotton and wool that the baby would be wrapped in. Another went to stoke up the fire and fill a hot water bottle. She came back shortly in distress to tell me that in filling the bottle, it had burst. Rubber perishes easily in tropical climates. And, she explained, it was our last hot water bottle. As in the west it is no good crying over spilt milk, so in Central Africa it might be considered no good crying over burst water bottles. They do not grow on trees and there are no drugstores down forest pathways.

"Alright," I said, "put the baby as near the fire as safely as you can and sleep between the baby and the door to keep it from drafts. Your job is to keep the baby warm."

The following noon, as I did most days, I went to have prayers with any of the orphanage children who chose to gather with me. I have the youngsters' various suggestions of things to pray about and told about the tiny baby. I explained our problem about keeping the baby warm enough, mentioned the hot water bottle and that the baby could so easily die if it got chills. I also told them of the two-year-old sister crying because her mother had died. During prayer time, one ten-year-old girl Ruth prayed with the usual blunt conciseness of our African children. "Please God," she prayed, "Send us a hot water bottle today. It'll be no good tomorrow, God, as the baby will be dead—so please send it this afternoon."

While I had gasped at the audacity of the prayer, she added, "And while you're about it would you please send a dolly for the little girl so she'll know you really love her?" As often with children's prayers I was put on the spot: could I honestly say Amen? *I just didn't believe that God could do this. Oh yes, I know that He can do everything. The Bible says so. But there are limits, aren't there? The only way God could answer this particular prayer would be by sending me a parcel from the homeland. I had been in Africa for almost four years at that time and I had never ever received a parcel from home. Anyway, if anyone did send me a parcel, who would put a hot water bottle in it? I lived on the equator.*

Halfway through the afternoon while I was teaching in the nurses' training school, a message was sent that there was a car at my front door. By the time I reached home the car had gone but there on the veranda was a large 22lb. parcel. I felt tears pricking my eyes; I could not open the parcel alone so I sent for the orphanage children.

Together we pulled off the string, carefully undid each knot; we folded the paper, taking care not to tear it unduly. Excitement was mounting. Some 30 or 40 pairs of eyes were focused on the large cardboard box. From the top I lifted out a brightly colored knitted jersey, eyes sparkled as I gave them out. There were the knitting bandages for the leprosy patients. The children looked a little bored then came a bottle of mixed raisins and saltines that would make a bunch of buns for the weekend. Then as I put my hand in again I felt the ... could it really be ... I grasped it and pulled it out; yes, a brand new rubber hot water bottle. I cried. I had not asked God to send it. I had not truly believed that He would.

Ruth was in the front row of the children. She rushed forward crying out, "If God has sent the bottle He must have send the dolly too." Rummaging down to the bottom of the box she pulled out a small, beautifully dressed dolly. Her eyes shone. She had never doubted. Looking up at me she asked, "Can I go over with you and give this dolly to this little girl so she'll know that Jesus really loves her?"

"Of course," I replied.

That parcel had been on the way for five whole months, packed up by my former Sunday school class whose leader had heard and obeyed God's prompting to send a hot water bottle, even to the equator. And one of the girls had put in a doll for an African child five months before—an answer to the believing prayer of a ten-year-old to bring it that afternoon.

Isaiah 65:24 says, *"Before they call, I will answer; while they are still speaking I will hear."* God is always listening, and He always has an answer. He has a plan, and it's always a good one. All things are possible with Him! Many of us pray when we first get saved, but that's the last conversation we have with Him. But He wants so much more relationship with us! As the verse in Isaiah shows us, He is intimately connected to us—and wants to stay that way.

As we're setting our financial goals and plans and going about working them out, it's important that we stay connected to God. It's important that we submit our plans to Him always. Proverbs 16:4 tells us, *"Commit to the Lord whatever you do, and he will establish your plans."* Even as you're budgeting and saving and working out your plans, daily recommit them to the Lord. Stay in close relationship with Him. He has all the answers, all the provision, and all the open doors you need!

As with all relationships, we need to cultivate this one. What are some ways we can do that? In 1 Timothy 4:8, Paul writes, *"Physical training is of some value, but godliness has value for all things, holding promise for both the present life and the life to come."* In other words, in the same way you would exercise your physical body and make a plan for that, you can and should have a spiritual exercise plan.

Have a daily plan for what that might look like. Here are some suggestions:

- There's a saying that goes like this: "Be the kind of person that when your feet hit the floor, Satan says, "Oh darn, (s)he's up and at it again!" Use your days to fight the good fight, to do God's work—and to stay conscious of your relationship with Him. Start your day with a reminder of that reality: "God, I'm here for You today! What's the plan?"

- Reading scripture is very important. If we want to get to know God's voice, it helps to know what that might sound like. Reading our Bible teaches us about God's character, and about how He speaks. Learn to use a concordance, as you study various topics. Even starting with spending 10-15 minutes a day in the Word will make a difference in how you approach each day.

- Be a good steward of your day! Make a plan for each day, with specific slots for each activity:

maybe half an hour for social media, half an hour for exercise, an hour for household tasks, things like that. Then use a timer, and stick to your plan!

- Pray and worship throughout your day. Perhaps take a few minutes during your lunch or coffee break to spend some time in worship and prayer. I've known folks who go sit in their car on their breaks and turn on their favorite worship CD for a few minutes. It serves to turn their heart back to God in the middle of the day.

- Take a few minutes at the end of the day and do a little heart inventory. Ask God questions like, "Did I do the best I could today? Are we connected? Did I trust You? Is there anyone I need to forgive?"

As you begin to intentionally set your heart on God throughout the day, you'll notice a difference in many areas of your life. You'll see the fruit of it in your relationships, in your overall well-being, and very likely in the area of your finances. Which is our point in going through this book, isn't it?

HOMEWORK:

1. Set some time in your schedule every day to pray, if you don't already. Many people like begin their day with prayer. Try getting up 15 minutes earlier than normal, and commit to spending that time with God.

Look for a devotional to help, if you'd like. There are many good ones out there! Remember, though, that your good Father just wants to talk to you, and have you talk to Him!

2. Create a prayer journal, in addition to your Gratitude Journal. Begin to note areas of prayer, and then mark the date when God answers your prayers!

3. Assess:
   Where are you now in your:
   - Spending Tracker

     By now, you should have a pretty steady habit of tracking your spending. Examine any ways you can get better; maybe you've forgotten about any online recurring charges for subscriptions.

     Take some time and check those things, and evaluate if you need to make any changes.

   - Gratitude Journal

     How are you doing, keeping up with this journal? What differences do you notice in your attitude? Go ahead and journal those differences, right there in your Gratitude Journal!

     Consider adding more items to your daily list. You can never be too grateful!

   - Goals

How are you progressing with your SMART goals? Other goals? Take some time this week and evaluate your progress. Make Any updates needed. For example, have you realized that your "Realistic" goals need a little tweaking in order to *really* be realistic? Make any necessary changes to your plan.

CHAPTER 10 - Working Together

*"That is why a man leaves his father and mother and is
united to his wife, and they become one flesh."*
Genesis 2:24

PRAYER: *Lord, thank You for my spouse. Thank You for
our life together! Help us to grow together as we learn to
be good stewards. Help us to honor one another in our
choices and in our attitudes. Help us find joy in each other,
and in You! Amen.*

Chances are, you're not doing this budget thing on your
own. Even if you are single, this is still an important
chapter to read! Don't skip it!

If you're this far into this book, you've made something
of a commitment to analyzing and changing your
financial situation. That's a wonderful thing! You will see
fruit from that, I have no doubt!

But, you say, it's not just me that needs to dig into this.

If you're married, as many of you are, this journey to
financial freedom will be (or should be) a joint effort—as
with anything else in your relationship. God said that a
man will leave his parents and be joined to his wife, and
the two would become one. Many of you will have joint
bank accounts and operate out of the same budget, so it's
important to sit down together and get on the same page.
One of the biggest sources of conflict in marriage seems
to be finances. Sometimes it's a philosophical issue, but
more often than not it's a communication issue. We
haven't communicated our priorities and expectations
clearly enough, and most of us assume that everyone is

like us, so why wouldn't our spouse think the same way we do about this too? Then things happen, we get our feelings hurt, we fight—and then we're disconnected.

There are several types of money personalities, depending on the author. There are approximately six. You will find some authors have more and some less. Much of our life does revolve around money and how we handle money is really a function of who we really are. This includes our core personality – our core personality traits and our life experiences. How we grew up and where we grew up.

One of the personality types will tend to be more predominant than the other. Understanding which personality type best fits us is important. It has an impact on how we relate to God, others and how we deal with our money matters.

The personality types are as follows:

- Personality type number one is *the slob*. These individuals find it very difficult to get organized. They have a fair amount of clutter, which often means their financial life is chaotic (when you don't know what you have, you often buy things again and again). There usually isn't a budget. This can be a great source of problems within a marriage; if one partner just is scattered all over the place, you may need a bit of stability. It's important to find out which of you can keep the two of you grounded. I'm not talking about getting out there with a whip, hurting people and putting them down when using this as a tool. Do not hurt, demise or put someone down. We're using this idea of "grounding" as a tool to lift each other up! It's like being an alcoholic; you have to recognize you are an alcoholic first before you can make steps to change. The same is true for the financial slob; they need to admit a budget is needed to move forward.

- The second personality type is *the people person.* Relationships mean everything and it's difficult for them to manage their financial goals and to see that finances should be a priority in their life. They are the type that would say, "Don't bother me with all those details." She or he often is very generous to a fault. While people person traits can be very endearing, they can also lead to some problems similar to the slob. Realizing finances should be a priority is low on the list for this group since there's often too much going on for them to be really grounded financially.

- Type number three is *the spender.* There is often tremendous short-term emotional satisfaction when buying things for him or herself. They spend more than they have and they usually don't think about the consequences down the line. This then tends to lead to debt.

- Type number four is *the hoarder.* Think about a squirrel. These folks are like squirrels with their money. They stash it away. It's not necessarily for appropriate means and it's often done out of a desire to develop a sense of security. It also borders on being stingy.

- Type number five is *the winner.* This group considers money a game. They want to stay ahead of the Jones' so they play to win. Often it is subliminal accomplishments that are important to this person. Their drive needs to be tempered by a motive of love rather than the desire to be number one.

- The last type of person we have on the list is *the penny pincher*. This is an individual who uses coupons, watches for the specials, but they fail to look at the big picture. They may use the coupons but they still may overspend because sometimes people get stuff on sale and go to the bookstore when it's not really appropriate. It's a good deal, but do we really need it or will it perish and not be usable in the end. And in the end if it perishes, it isn't a good deal. This person also may not make good decisions based on Godly priorities; for example, education for their children.

The various personalities are a result of how we were raised, and our experiences with money growing up. There's no real formula either; people who came from lower income families can be hoarders or penny pinchers, or big spenders. People raised with plenty of resources may be slobs (lack of appreciation, maybe?)— or they can be very disciplined with their money. But our experiences and the attitudes of the people who raised us tend to form our financial personalities.

The media also seems to have an impact on many people these days, especially on young people who have been raised with television and the Internet. Amazon makes it easy to shop for anything your heart desires, and you don't even have to get out of your pajamas! Everything from food to clothes to diapers and more can be at your house in a matter of hours, with just the click of a button. With this kind of ease and access, it's no wonder so many people find themselves in financial trouble!

These personalities will shape who we are, how we raise our children, the impact we have on our friends, and the choices we make about how we spend our money.

But understanding how attitudes develop isn't as important as learning how to modify them when necessary. Remember we can always change; but change takes time. We didn't get where we are today overnight, nor will we make lasting changes quickly.

It's crucial to the health of your marriage, if you haven't done it already, to discuss your budget, your spending, and your individual financial personality types. Be honest with yourself, and ask your spouse to be honest with you. Then work to get those possibly very different personalities on the same page.

I have been married for more than 30 years, and I can tell you that there are many times you will not be on the same page. I saw it in my parents' marriage, I've seen it in mine, and I've seen it in plenty of other marriages. I've seen it in the couples sitting across from me, looking for financial counseling. It's impossible to agree on everything 100% of the time because we are all individuals. Different individuals, with unique experiences and perspectives.

This is why it's crucial to *talk.* Communicate. Ask questions, and be open about your feelings. It's important to talk about the big things (see this chapter's homework for a discussion guide), but it's also important to talk about the little things.

My husband and I had agreed on a specific budget, with what I thought were clear boundaries. One night, he took my daughter out to eat (a wonderful thing!). I didn't have a problem with that—but I had a problem with the fact that the liquor bill was equal to the food bill, and there was only one person drinking! The smart thing to do would have been to bring it up with him right then and there, but I didn't say anything.

A couple of weeks later, my husband asked me if I was wearing new blue jeans; I was. He let me know they weren't in the budget; I responded with, "Well, neither was the dinner with all the alcohol."

Ouch.

Clearly we needed to communicate with each other, and clearly I needed to work on my attitude. I realized that I was annoyed with him for not consulting with me, and I justified purchasing new jeans with a "he did it too" kind of attitude. We ended up talking it out and we got through it just fine, but it would have been better if we had communicated on the front end!

I've read statistics that say money is one of the top causes of divorce. I would say it's not money itself, but failure to communicate well about money that would be a reason people divorce. Not being on the same page can easily lead to hurt feelings and fights, like the one my husband and I had.

It seemed like that fight was about alcohol and jeans, but it was really about how we didn't communicate with each other. I wasn't clear about my expectations regarding our "eating out" budget; I just assumed he would "know." And instead of talking to him about it right then, as soon as I was upset, I let it fester and build and cause disconnection. He didn't communicate any expectations about buying jeans, and then got upset when I didn't tell him.

Although a pair of jeans was what brought things to the surface, the actual fight was about other things. I felt hurt when he spent that much money on alcohol; he felt hurt when I bought jeans without talking about it first.

Communication is the primary way we connect with each other. There are two kinds of communication: overt and covert. Overt communication is the words I say; covert communication is everything else. It's said that 90% of our communication is non-verbal: body language, behavior, etc. When my husband spent too much money on alcohol, it seemed as if he were telling me he didn't value me. And when I bought jeans without discussing it, I communicated the same to him. Not with words, but with our actions.

We often get hurt in relationships when our covert and our overt messages don't match. Although I had told my husband I loved him, probably even the day I bought those jeans, my actions communicated something else— whether I meant them to or not. So money was the catalyst, but we clearly had some things to work on.

(We did, and we're just fine now—in case you were wondering!)

This week's homework is designed to help you and your spouse get on the same page about your finances. Keep in mind that every couple is different, and each couple's way of working these things out will be different. Your main goal is always connection!

HOMEWORK:

This week's homework is all about connecting you and your spouse. Money is the topic at hand, but remember that the ultimate goal is not about dollars and cents, but about taking care of your relationship!

1. Go back to the section on personalities in this chapter. Honestly assess which one you are; allow your spouse to do the same. Let them do a self-assessment before you discuss.

2. When you've figured out your own financial personality, identify some ways that you may need to adjust. Where can you grow? What changes can you make—before you meet with your spouse—to begin to address your own issues?

3. Once you've done that, schedule a meeting with your spouse. Consider planning a night where you can sit together at the kitchen table or at a coffee shop (if it fits into your budget!!). Don't plan to talk about money on a night when the kids have to be 10 different directions at once, dinner got burned, Grandma is at the house, etc. Make every effort to be calm and peaceful when you get together!

4. Take some time and discuss your thoughts about *you*. It's important to begin this process with focusing on yourself before you discuss your

spouse. Really work to her what he or she is saying about themselves before you jump in with your opinions.

5. If your opinion differs from his or hers, ask if you can share your thoughts. Be willing and open to your spouse's thoughts being different than yours—even about how they see themselves!

6. Take some time and explore together how you can support each other as you change and grow. Remember, your spouse doesn't need to be just like you, and you don't need to be just like him or her!

7. Don't tackle too much at the first meeting. Schedule a second meeting, perhaps for the following week, when you can discuss creating a budget. Start with the **Personal Cash Position** worksheet in the Appendix, if you haven't used it already. At your second meeting, sit down together and go over this worksheet.

8. Then, using the **Debt to Income Ratio** worksheet, get a realistic idea of where you are financially as a couple and/or as a family. Using this sheet will give you a very clear idea of where changes need to be made.

9. Move on to the **Preparing the Plan** worksheet, using the information in the other two. Decide together what areas you're going to work on.

10. Using your **SMART** goals from Chapter 8, set a financial goal together. For example, maybe you've discovered that your housing debt ratio is too high, and you need to adjust your housing costs. Together, create a plan to begin to move in the direction you want.

11. Plan monthly meetings (or weekly, if you can) with just you and your spouse to check in: how is

your plan going? Are you working the plan you both agreed on? What adjustments need to be made?

12. When you're done with each meeting, take some time and connect. Take a walk together, and hold hands. Talk about the weather, a book you're reading … something just meant for connection. Have some ice cream. Play a game. Do something that reminds you why you're working on your finances to begin with!

**It's important to recognize when we need some help in our marriage. There's no shame at all in getting some counseling, whether it's for relationship stuff, financial stuff, parenting, or whatever, if you find that you need it, get some help! It will be worth it!

CHAPTER 11 - Money and Our Kids

"Start children off on the way they should go, and even when they are old they will not turn from it."
Proverbs 22:6

PRAYER: *Lord, thank You for my child(ren). Thank You for their unique gifts and talents, for the amazing way You designed them. Help me to remember that they won't be children forever, and help me raise wise and generous adults who love You and follow you, all the days of their lives. Thank You for providing for our family! Amen.*

I knew a young lady who went off to university one September, with some new bedding, a few posters, and a checking account—which she knew nothing about. She had pretty rainbow colored checks, and apparently all she would need to do to get pizza every night was to sign her name on that bottom line.

Three weeks in to the school year, she got a call from her mother, asking why the bank was calling—informing her parents about multiple "overdrawn" charges. The young lady was baffled. How could such a thing have happened? She only bought some chips one week, and some pizza a few times ... oh, and there was that time she and her roommate went to the mall and bought a new shirt. Or two. And the extra books her professor had *required* them to buy for class ... ok, maybe not *required*, but he suggested strongly that they have these books. So she bought them.

The young lady's mother realized she had done her daughter a great disservice. They had sent her off to school with money—and no idea how to handle it.

Training our children in regards to money must begin early in their lives. From a very young age, children can learn the value of money and stewardship—and who better to teach them, than mom and dad?

Young children can be taught about money. Hand a young child one dollar, take her to the grocery, and help her discover what that dollar will buy. When she's a little older, have her help with grocery lists and food budgets. When your son asks for a toy, tell him how much it's going to cost (not his birthday presents; don't do that with his birthday presents). Sit with him for a few minutes, and compare: what other things cost that amount? What food? Clothing?

Many people think this is sort of a "scare tactic," that it's introducing ideas and responsibilities before a child is ready. I disagree. I think that many of the issues adults bring into my office stem from not knowing the value of a dollar. Most children have no idea what things cost. They really think that mommy and daddy have unlimited funds, and can buy anything they, the child, want. When mommy and daddy say no, little Johnny gets mad because he doesn't understand that mommy and daddy aren't saying no because they're mean; they're saying no because they need to pay the electric bill.

Young children can be taught the concept that saying "yes" to one thing means saying "no" to another. They can and should begin to understand that things cost money, even the hot dog they had for lunch. Include little ones in things like meal planning and grocery shopping. When my children were little, they loved to sit in the cart while I shopped; many grocery stores had small snacks like a banana or crackers for the kids, and they would listen as I read prices out loud. We would compare the value of one item versus another, and sometimes I would let them choose which one to buy.

School-aged children can be even more involved. Beginning fairly young, give kids a budget for school supplies and new school clothes. Allow them to decide what they need and what they don't need (check with your local schools; many schools now have required supply lists). Take them to the store with their budget, a list, and a calculator and guide them through the process of obtaining what they need.

Teenagers can go one step further. Give them an allowance for supplies and clothing—for the semester. If they spend it all at the beginning of semester, then they have to wait for the semester break to get new things.

In any of these situations, some children will naturally do better than others. Some will need more guidance and boundaries; they will try to push the envelope. Of course there will be things you will need to say no to; but there may be things your child wishes to buy that you would rather he not. This is a perfect learning opportunity! You may be tempted to clamp down and tell him no; resist! Instead, if the item isn't dangerous or illegal in some way, allow him to buy it. Then when he doesn't have enough left for the things he really needs, he will feel the sting of his choices. This is a valuable lesson, one he will never forget!

I recently went shopping with my own daughter for her school supplies. First, before we headed out the door to shop, I had her make a list of everything she needed this year. Then I had her go through what she already had at home. She compared the two lists, and this gave her a shopping list of needed items. Once we got to the store, she was ready to go. We stuck to her list, and were in and out of there in less than forty minutes, with everything she needed. She was happy, I was happy. All because we had a plan—and we stuck to it!

I had her do the same thing with respect to her clothing. At the beginning of the season, I had her go "shopping" in her own closet: what does she actually wear? What things had she forgotten about, that she could wear again. What had she outgrown?

I've found that sometimes it's helpful to have someone help you with this task. We tend to be sentimental about clothes, even when they're out of style or no longer fit. A different set of eyes can help us be more objective about what to keep and what to get rid of.

When your teens are cleaning out their closets, they might need a balance of some coaching and some space. Remind them that this is for their benefit, as they are about to go shopping! (And don't think this is only for the girls; many teenage boys are very selective about their clothing, and would love the opportunity to choose things for themselves!)

Some areas now have resale shops that target young people. Check your local area to see if such a thing exists near you. Make an offer to your teen, that if they will take their discarded clothes to the resale shop, you will add whatever they get to their shopping budget. Two birds with one stone!

With my daughter, we went through her list: "This is what I have, this is what I need, this is what I would like." We also set a dollar limit.

Next, with that dollar limit we went to the bank and withdrew the cash. Everywhere we went, we only paid cash. That way, when the cash ran out, we would know that our shopping trip was over. My daughter could watch the amount decreasing as we went from place to place, and she would know exactly how much she had left. As we purchased the shoes, she saw the five $20s go out. When we bought the t-shirts and jeans, she could actually see the stack of bills get smaller. It was a great way to measure what was being spent.

On her own, she had gone to one of the warehouse outlet stores. She said, "You know, Mom, I can get a really nice graphic t-shirt here for $5." The same thing happened with jeans; she found great quality jeans at a fraction of the price of what they would have cost at the mall.

She was so excited about her experience, and it was a great exercise for her—and for me. One of my personal shortcomings is that I tend to be something of a shopaholic. As I watched my daughter's shopping experience, I realized that I could do the same thing. So the next season, I went through my closet just the way she had. I did exactly what she had done, and I found myself in a strange position: I really didn't need anything.

Our children will eventually grow up and become adults (at least, that's the plan). One of the primary ways we can set them up for success is by handing them healthy attitudes and effective tools for dealing with money. There is absolutely no reason not to use the principles laid out in this book and the worksheets from the Appendix with your children, especially as they head off to university—or better yet, when they graduate from university and are about to establish their own homes.

What about university, you ask? Should we as parents pay for it, or not? That's not an easy question to answer. As you go through the exercises in Chapter 10, it would be good to add that subject to the list. Decide together how you feel about higher education, and if you can and should help your children access it.

It's good to remember that in these times, a degree doesn't always guarantee a job the way it did when most of us were growing up. I'm not looking at the glass half empty here; I'm being realistic. You and I both know people who have degrees—and their jobs have nothing to do with that degree.

Of course there is value in education. The process of beginning and completing a degree plan is nothing to scoff at, and employers do look at that sort of thing. But there are other (often less expensive) options for learning skills and gaining experience. Look into apprenticeships for your high school students. Find volunteer opportunities. Encourage your children to explore creative ways to develop their skills, talents and interests.

If you decide that college is the way to go, begin saving as soon as possible. Tuition and other costs are rising rapidly, so it's in your and your child's best interest to begin the process as early as possible. There are programs available that allow you to "lock in" certain tuition prices; explore options in your area.

What about inheritance? How much should we leave to our children? That, my friends, is entirely up to you.

Let's look at what scripture says. Proverbs 13:22 says, *"A good person leaves an inheritance for his children's children."* It's biblical to provide for future generations! Imagine your grandchildren (or your future grandchildren) having access to resources you didn't have at their age. Would it help them to be able to purchase a new car, or a house, or even have an extra few hundred dollars? Of course it would. Just like it would have helped you.

I see motor homes on the highway with bumper stickers that say, "We're spending our kids' inheritance." Of course the money is yours to do with what you want to, but what kind of a legacy are you leaving for your children? So many people leave their kids with a legacy of debt and poverty, when with a little planning, they could have left something very, very different. Inheritance isn't about an amount; it's about what you're leaving behind. Generosity, wealth, and abundance? Or poverty, lack, and overspending?

Once you've decided how you're going to handle inheritance, it's important to make sure that you have your Will and Estate Plan completed. You may think, well, I don't have very much, so why is it so important? If you don't decide how you want your money spent after you die, the government will decide for you.

Even more importantly, your Will and Estate Plan will document where your children should go, if they are under the age of 16. Once they are 16, they can choose where they go. (This law varies by location, so it's a good idea to check this information with an attorney as you are drawing up your plan.) Discuss with your spouse who might be a good guardian for your children in the event they should need it, and then discuss it with those folks. It's good to get their agreement before you add it to a legal document!

Consider discussing a trust fund for your children. Proverbs 20:21 says, *"An inheritance claimed too soon will not be blessed at the end."* In other words, too much too soon could be harmful to your kids rather than helpful. As we know, kids still need help managing their money well into adulthood; we read story after story of a young person coming into too much money—and blowing it. So the idea of a trust fund that would provide for them while not overwhelming them might be a good idea.

Ultimately, the question of money and your children is this: What legacy am I leaving them? Am I preparing them, both by instruction and inheritance, to be successful adults? If not, how can I start? Don't wait—start today!

HOMEWORK:

1. Decide how to begin preparing your children for adulthood. Are they still little? Using the tips listed in this chapter, pick 2 ways you can begin to train them up in the area of money. Use those tips this week.

2. If your children are older, perhaps teenagers, begin to bring them into discussions about budgeting and saving. Allow them to speak into family matters, and include them in planning, where appropriate.
3. Introduce the idea of a Gratitude Journal to your children, no matter what age. Offer to help pick one out, and then show them how to use it. You're never too young to learn to be grateful!
4. If you don't have a Will and Estate Plan, begin that process now. Set a goal to find out exactly how to do that in your area; have the information by the end of the week.
5. If your children are older, show them the documents in the Appendix and teach them how to use them. Make them a copy, and have them start tracking their expenditures.

CHAPTER 12 - Final Steps

PRAYER: *Lord, thank You for everything in my life. Thank You for leading and guiding, for providing, and for teaching me to steward Your good gifts in my life. May I learn to love You well, through loving others well. Help me to use the gifts You have given me—my time, my talents, and my treasure—in the service of others. Help me to be a reflection of Your glory in everything I do. Amen.*

Back in my college days, I won a scholarship. The night it was presented to me, the keynote speaker told me something I've never forgotten. She said, "I know you'll probably want to spend this money on books or school supplies. But I encourage you to take a small part of this award that you've received and buy yourself a memento, something that will remind you every time you look at it of what you've achieved. Let it remind you that yes, you reached success once, and yes, you can do it again."

I took her advice. I went out and bought a ring that I still have, to this day. Every time I wear it I'm reminded that I have the potential to do great things.

You do, too.

You can do this. You can, with God's help and some work, achieve your financial goals. I believe in you.

It's important to celebrate your successes as you go. Let the times where your hard work pays off remind you that there is success in the future too. Use your tracking tools and your journals as evidence of God's faithfulness in your life. Refer to them again and again, whenever you need some encouragement. And feel free to come back to this book time and time again, and use the principles in it!

We will end where we began. God is a good Father, who has only good things in store for you. His desire is that you and He would steward those things together, hand in hand, along your journey. It's a lifelong journey, but one with generational—and even eternal—rewards. It's well worth the effort, wouldn't you say?

APPENDIX 1 - Personal Cash Position

Personal Cash Position

	Jan	Jan Actual	Feb	Feb actual
INCOME				
Base Income				
Bonus				
Spouse Income				
Rent				
Income tax Refunds				
Gifts				

Total Income

INVESTMENTS				
RRSP				
Spouse RRSP				
RESP				
Real Estate				
Stocks				

Total Investments

HOUSING				
Mortgage				
Insurance				
Maintenance				

Property Taxes				
Hydro				
Telephone				
Gas				
Furnace / Hot Water Rental				
Cable TV				
Water				
Miscellaneous				
Total Housing				

AUTOMOBILES

Leases	His				
	Hers				
Insurance					
Gas					
Maintenance					
Toll Roads					
Licenses					

Total Automobile

SCHOOL

Tuition Fees				
Field Trips / Drama				
Uniforms				
Cast				
Lunches				

EXTRA ACTIVITIES

Dance	Regular classes				
	Small group fees				
	Costumes				
	Miscellaneous				
Horseback Riding					
Soccer					
Summer Activities					

Total Extra Activities

GENERAL EXPENSES

Groceries				
Liquor				
Medical/Dental				
Charities				
Gifts				
Vacation				
Interest Expense (Non-mortgage)				
Eating out				
Housecleaning				
Life Insurance				
Miscellaneous				
Staples				
Church - tithing				
Cleaners				
Michael's				

Dog food					
Clothes					
Gym					
Books					
Sponsorship					
Running rm					
CDN tire					
Trip					
Lunch - his					
Lunch - hers					

Total General Expenses

Total Expenses

Residual Net Income

APPENDIX 2 - Exercising Our Faith in God

This week I will:

Action Item	This Week's Strategy
I will stop worrying about … I will hand it over to God to take care of and I will dwell on the things that are pure, wholesome, joyful and of good report.	
I will ask God for … I will remember that "all things are possible through God."	
I will Trust God to meet my every need in the following situation…	
I will allow God to do His work in this situation …	
I will consciously pray about …… when I am …	

James 1:17 says, *"Every good and perfect gift is from above, coming down from the Father of the heavenly lights, who does not change like shifting shadows."* Do you see what that says? *Every* gift. Every single one. There's nothing that we have that didn't come from our heavenly

Father. Romans tells us that *"from him and through him and to him are all things* (Romans 11:36). From Him are all things!!

Notice that it says in James that every *good* gift comes from the Father of Lights. You see, we have a very, very good Father, who desires to give us *good things.* Proverbs 10:23 says, *"The blessing of the Lord brings wealth, and he adds no trouble to it."* We have a very generous heavenly Father, who blesses us with wealth! The same Father who knows exactly how many hairs we have on our heads (Luke 12:7) provides everything we need. He is the one who provided all that stuff you have in your garages and closets!

I know many of you may have had negative experiences with your earthly father, but it's so important to know just how good our heavenly Father is. Earlier, I quoted the book of James, which tells us that *"every good and perfect gift"* comes from Him! His heart is to give you good things, to fill your life with blessings. He is an abundant, gift-giving Father.

Although He loves us and wants good things for us, His heart is not that we would become hoarders of things, overloaded and overstuffed with *stuff.* One way we can know this is true is that *you can't take it with you when you go.* Any of it. All of us will die someday, and when we do, all of our stuff stays right here.

The Egyptians provide us with a great example of this. In ancient Egyptian culture, when someone died, he or she was often buried with many of his or her favorite possessions: furniture, pots, bowls, clothing. One pharaoh was even buried with a boat! And how do we know they didn't take it with them when they died? Well, the fact that archaeologists were able to dig it up thousands of years later proves that while the person buried in the tomb had gone on to eternity, his or her possessions were still right here on earth.

So if we're not to hoard them, and we can't take them with us, what are we to do with our generous God's abundant blessings? Read this story from Matthew 25:

14 "Again, it will be like a man going on a journey, who called his servants and entrusted his wealth to them. 15 To one he gave five bags of gold, to another two bags, and to another one bag, each according to his ability. Then he went on his journey. 16 The man who had received five bags of gold went at once and put his money to work and gained five bags more. 17 So also, the one with two bags of gold gained two more. 18 But the man who had received one bag went off, dug a hole in the ground and hid his master's money.

19 "After a long time the master of those servants returned and settled accounts with them. 20 The man who had received five bags of gold brought the other five. 'Master,' he said, 'you entrusted me with five bags of gold. See, I have gained five more.'

21 "His master replied, 'Well done, good and faithful servant! You have been faithful with a few things; I will put you in charge of many things. Come and share your master's happiness!'

22 "The man with two bags of gold also came. 'Master,' he said, 'you entrusted me with two bags of gold; see, I have gained two more.'

23 "His master replied, 'Well done, good and faithful servant! You have been faithful with a few things; I will put you in charge of many things. Come and share your master's happiness!'

²⁴ "Then the man who had received one bag of gold came. 'Master,' he said, 'I knew that you are a hard man, harvesting where you have not sown and gathering where you have not scattered seed. ²⁵ So I was afraid and went out and hid your gold in the ground. See, here is what belongs to you.'

²⁶ "His master replied, 'You wicked, lazy servant! So you knew that I harvest where I have not sown and gather where I have not scattered seed? ²⁷ Well then, you should have put my money on deposit with the bankers, so that when I returned I would have received it back with interest.

²⁸ "'So take the bag of gold from him and give it to the one who has ten bags. ²⁹ For whoever has will be given more, and they will have an abundance. Whoever does not have, even what they have will be taken from them. ³⁰ And throw that worthless servant outside, into the darkness, where there will be weeping and gnashing of teeth.'

The man who buried his treasure lost everything. (It's also important to notice that he was the man who called the Master a "hard man;" he did not understand the Father's generous heart!) We are to *steward* God's blessings, multiplying them and distributing them to others.

Our very generous Father takes this pretty seriously. Read what Proverbs has to say: *"Whoever shuts their ears to the cry of the poor will also cry out and not be answered"* (Proverbs 21:13). What would it mean to "shut our ears" to the cry of the poor? It would mean not using our resources to help others less fortunate than we are. When He gives us things, He intends for us to use those things to bless others and advance his Kingdom. He blesses us so that we in turn can be a blessing to others.

God also asks us to give back to our local church body; we call it "tithing." The principle of tithing looks like this: God gives us 100% of what we have, and asks that we return 10% of it back to our church.

But God is so good, that even in asking us to tithe, He makes us promises! Look at this: *"Bring the whole tithe into the storehouse, that there may be food in my house. Test me in this," says the LORD Almighty, "and see if I will not throw open the floodgates of heaven and pour out so much blessing that there will not be room enough to store it. I will prevent pests from devouring your crops, and the vines in your fields will not drop their fruit before it is ripe," says the LORD Almighty. "Then all the nations will call you blessed, for yours will be a delightful land," says the LORD Almighty"* (Malachi 3:10). When we follow his instructions to tithe on what He's given us, he will open the floodgates of heaven!

This is also the one area where God gives us permission to "test" Him: *"see if I won't do it,"* He says. Nowhere else are we commanded to test Him and His faithfulness. But in this area, He actually invites us to do it!

You may be wondering, "What is a *tithe?*" A tithe is defined as $1/10^{th}$ of your income, given back to the Lord. Leviticus 27:30 says, *"A tithe of everything from the land, whether grain from the soil or fruit from the trees, belongs to the LORD; it is holy to the LORD."* Most people believe it should be the first tenth, the first thing you do with your money after getting paid. We'll talk more about it later in this book, but Scripture shows us that because God is a good God, and everything comes from Him, that we should return a portion of it to Him.

You see, everything we have comes from God, and is to be returned to Him to be used for His purposes. It's all His anyway!

Throughout this book, we will examine God's heart about money—and our own. We will dig into our money personalities, our budgets (or lack thereof), our savings plans, and how we can leave a legacy for the next generation. It will be hard sometimes; we tend to get a little weird about money, don't we? We don't like people digging into our finances, or our heart about them. We may get defensive, and you may ask, "Who are you, Margaret, to ask me all these questions about *my money?*"

If you're reading this book, it's likely because you've found yourself in a place where you absolutely have to examine your finances. Maybe you're in a crisis, and you don't know how to get out. Or maybe you're not in crisis yet—but you know you're headed for one.

Or maybe you're just starting out in life, and you're ready to build a foundation of financial security. Wherever you are, we're on this journey together. Today is the first day of your future!

Ready? Let's go!

HOMEWORK:

Matthew 6:21 says, *"For where your treasure is, there your heart will be also."* We've quoted that backwards sometimes, thinking that what we love is where we will spend our money or time or energy. And that's true, but if you look at what the actual verse says, it shows that we can look at where we spend our time or money or energy to find out where our heart is!

In the Appendix of this book, you will find a worksheet entitled **"Personal Cash Position."** This worksheet is designed to give you a snapshot of where you are financially, right now.

For your homework this week, take the worksheet and your personal bank statement and begin to categorize your spending. Make sure you're categorizing not just your credit or debit card expenditures, but your cash spending. If you don't normally track your cash spending, now would be a good time to begin to track that.

I suggest getting a small notebook, and beginning to track all of your spending. Make sure you write down everything—that cup of coffee at the gas station, the quick run through the drive-thru, the extra magazine at the grocery store. You might be surprised at how much you're spending at Tim Horton's or Starbucks, a dollar here or five dollars there. It adds up!

About The Author

Margaret L. Good has transformed lives by showing people that success, wealth and living abundantly is not difficult when you learn simple life altering principles. She is an Amazon and Barnes and Nobel three-time best-selling co-author, coach and speaker. She was crowned the #1 Independent Sales Consultant in Mary Kay Canada in July 2017 out of 37,000 consultants Canada wide. She has hosted her own radio program "God's Financial Plan on Joy 1250 AM.

For close to 40 years, Margaret has supported hundreds of people from many walks of life as a Chartered Professional Accountant. Margaret is a unique and stand-alone speaker and coach. Her candor and ability to point out what your true gifts, talents and inspirations are. By doing so, she can quickly help you live the life you have always dreamed of.

Helping you reach your fullest potential is Margaret's mission in life. A stellar businesswoman, wife and mother, Margaret shows her clients and audiences how to truly have it all and live the way you want to, aligned with God and never in scarcity.

Margaret continues to support local charities with her financial literacy program and the donation of her time and talents.

www.ingramcontent.com/pod-product-compliance
Lightning Source LLC
Chambersburg PA
CBHW071004040426
42443CB00007B/652